EXETER

By the same author

THE BUILDING OF BATH
CHELTENHAM
THE THREE CHOIRS CITIES

1   Exeter: The West Front of the Cathedral, 1346-75

EXETER

*Crediton, Cullompton, Exmouth,
Ottery St. Mary, Tiverton and Topsham*

Bryan Little

London
B. T. BATSFORD LTD

First Published, 1953

MADE AND PRINTED IN GREAT BRITAIN
BY JARROLD AND SONS LTD, LONDON AND NORWICH
FOR THE PUBLISHERS
B. T. BATSFORD LTD
HARDINGE STREET, PORTMAN SQUARE, LONDON, W.I

PREFACE

I HAVE never lived in Exeter, but am so much of the West country that the city has been to me an intimate, oft-repeated experience from my childhood days; I may fairly say that it is in my blood. The twin towers of the Cathedral impressed themselves on my earliest memories. There have been innumerable drives through Exeter, the shopping expeditions, the strolls through the older parts of the city, lunches and teas at the old Deller's with the car parked in Bedford Circus. There have been the walks by the Quay, the upward glances at carven intracacies of corbels and vaulted roof. Much of what I long knew has now disappeared, and Exeter will never be fully the same again, though its central area is more readily recognisable than central Plymouth. But there could be no more familiar or more congenial subject for me to describe; it is also possible that I have a blood link with the same Greenway family whose best known member was the great wool-man of Tiverton.

My book blends history and economics with architecture, and I have tried, as in works on other cities, to do equal justice to all that is important in the Exeter story—to the cloth trade and the secular buildings as well as to the city's stirring history and to the many mediaeval splendours of the Cathedral. Moreover, I have deliberately extended the book so as to make it a portrait, as well historical as of architecture, of the most important towns in a close-knit East Devon area whose central point is Exeter, but whose out-lying places are full of interest and greatly relevant to Exeter and to each other.

Though Exeter alone is a full and fascinating subject for a whole book, I have therefore widened my scope so as to take in the history and buildings of some other Devon towns that form so close a unity with their county town. For Exeter cannot well be considered in isolation; the whole of the lower basin of the Exe is a historic unity and shares in the same tradition of building and economic life. Moreover, though Ottery's river flows direct to the Channel, Bishop Grandisson, Coleridge, and William Gream the factory-builder all serve to link it to Exeter, Crediton, and Tiverton, and so to the whole fabric of this volume. My subject is therefore a compact unity, a cross whose hub is at Exeter itself and whose limbs end at Crediton, Tiverton, Ottery, and so through Raleigh's birthplace and Lady Nelson's grave to the Beacon and Dock of Exmouth.

My chosen towns also form a group whose intrinsic merits are great, and whose natives and residents have between them made up no inconsiderable proportion of England's famous men and women. For here in this book we see something, Exeter apart, of two minsters, two outstanding parish churches, two castles, England's oldest canal, some excellent domestic and industrial architecture, the leading West country Public School, and a pioneer among our western seaside resorts. There is a notable history of sieges and rebellions, there are literary associations with Thackeray and Black-more. Birthplaces include those of a great saint and a great poet, of two of our best miniaturists, of Sir Thomas Bodley and Sir Walter Raleigh.

My one regret is that I have had to treat my towns as it were like islands in the district, with little said on the intervening countryside. But I am not unaware either of its scenic and architectural merits or of the place it has filled in the story of Britain. One cannot pass lightly over a tract of country that gave birth to Raleigh, and whose place in our religious history is marked by Joanna Southcott born at Thorverton and George Gorham the eventual incumbent of Brampford Speke. It contains Whimple of cider fame and some important paper mills. Bradninch has history and a church of unusual note, the Aclands have in their various generations given significance to the area of Killerton, and the whole stretch of country between Topsham and Exmouth has some excellent Georgian architecture.

There are many to whom I owe a debt of gratitude for help and information during the preparation of this book. Among them I would mention the Dean of Exeter, Very Rev. A. Ross Wallace, D.D., the Cathedral Librarian, Miss M. P. Crighton, the City Librarian, Mr. N. S. E. Pugsley, and members of his staff, the City Architect of Exeter, Mr. H. B. Rowe, F.R.I.B.A., the

Deputy City Architect, Mr. E. B. Redfern, A.R.I.B.A., and Mr. A. L. Dennis, till recently on the staff of the Town Clerk. I also wish to thank Prof. E. J. Patterson, M.A., of Exeter. At Tiverton I had kind help from the Headmaster of Blundell's, Mr. J. S. Carter, M.A., and from Mr. S. A. Mahood, at Cullompton from the vicar, Rev. E. G. Hammond, M.A., and from Mrs. Nigel Neatby, and at Exmouth from Miss M. L. R. Tudor of A La Ronde. My thanks are also due to the curator of the Buckland Abbey Museum, near Plymouth, Mr. A. A. Cumming, F.M.A., to Mr. C. A. Raleigh Radford, F.R.Hist.Soc., F.S.A., and to Lt. Col. G. W. G. Hughes, D.S.O., of the Devonshire Association. Lastly, I have had frequent help from my good friends on the staff of the City Library at Bristol.

Clifton, Bristol   B.D.G.L.
March, 1953

ACKNOWLEDGMENT

THE Author and the Publishers wish to thank the following photographers for their permission to reproduce the illustrations in this book:
Aerofilms Ltd., for fig. 22; Chandler of Exeter, for fig. 59; Country Life Ltd., for fig. 56; the late Brian C. Clayton, for figs. 3, 4, 12 and 21; F. H. Crossley, for figs. 5, 11, 37 and 38; A. F. Kersting, F.R.P.S., for figs. 1, 6, 10, 13, 14, 16, 17, 23, 24, 26, 27, 32–36, 39–51, 53–55 and 58; Reece Winstone, A.R.P.S., for figs. 9, 25, 28–31, 52 and 57.

The maps, which appear as figs. 2 and 15, were specially drawn for the book by John P. Williams.

LIST OF ILLUSTRATIONS

BIBLIOGRAPHY

THE literature of Exeter is large, and I have been able neither to consult nor to list the whole of it; in addition to printed works there are the great quantities of MS material in civic and other possession at Exeter itself. Much of the printed material required for such a book as this can be found in works which deal with the county of Devon; these I have listed first. I have ventured to asterisk those which seem to me to be of special value.

DEVON

Tristram Risdon, *Survey of the County of Devon*, first publ. 1630; John Prince, *Worthies of Devon*, 1810; Rev. Richard Polwhele, *The History of Devonshire*, 1797; Rev. George Oliver, D.D., *Ecclesiastical Antiquities of Devon*, 1839, and *Monasticon Diocesis Exoniensis*, 1846; R. N. Worth, *A History of Devonshire*, 1886; John Stabb, *Some Old Devon Churches*, 3 vols., 1911; Nikolaus Pevsner, *South Devon* (The Buildings of England Series, Penguin Books), 1952*; Various Volumes of the *Transactions* of the Devonshire Association; see also Frances Rose-Troup, *The Western Rebellion of 1549*, 1913, and J. Britton and E. W. Brayley, *Devonshire Illustrated*, 1829; Leland, Celia Fiennes, and Defoe all have valuable descriptive matter.

EXETER

John Vowell, alias Hoker, *The Description of the City of Exeter*, c. 1580, ed. for the Devon and Cornwall Record Society, 1919 and 1947*; Richard Izacke, *Remarkable Antiquities of Exeter*, 1677, 3rd edn. by Samuel Izacke, 1724; Alexander Jenkins, *The History and Description of the City of Exeter*, 1806, 2nd edn., 1841*; Rev. George Oliver, D.D., *The History of Exeter*, 1861; Edward A. Freeman, *Exeter*, 1895; A. E. Richardson, *Regional Architecture in the West of England*, 1924 (refers also to other towns covered in this book); Thomas Sharp, *Exeter Phoenix*, 1946; W. G. Hoskins, article on Exeter in *History Today*, May 1951* and *Old Exeter*, 1952; *Architect's Journal*, August 21st, 1952* (for current building activity), and Eileen (Lady) Fox, *Roman Exeter*, 1952*.

For the Cathedral see Dugdale, *Monasticon*, vol. ii, *Some Account*

12

of the Cathedral Church of Exeter, ed. for Society of Antiquaries by Sir Henry Englefield, drawings by Carter, engravings by Basire, 1797*; John Britton, *The History and Antiquities of the Cathedral Church of Exeter*, 1826-7; Winkles, vol. ii, 1838. More modern works include Rev. George Oliver, D.D., *Lives of the Bishops of Exeter and a History of the Cathedral*, 1861; Percy Addleshaw, *Exeter* (Bell's series), 1898, revised 1899; W. R. Lethaby in the *Architectural Review*, 1903; A. Hamilton Thompson in the *Archaeological Journal* (dealing also with other Devon churches), 1913; Ethel Lega-Weekes, *Some Studies in the Topography of the Cathedral Close, Exeter*, 1915; H. E. Bishop and Edith K. Prideaux, *The Building of the Cathedral Church of St. Peter in Exeter*, 1922* (making use of the original fabric rolls); and Ven. A. H. Thompson, *The Cathedral Church of St. Peter in Exeter*, 1949*. For more detailed aspects of the Cathedral, see Edith K. Prideaux, *Figure Sculpture on the West front of Exeter Cathedral*, 1912; Miss K. M. Clarke, *The Misericords of Exeter Cathedral*, Devon and Cornwall N. & Q., vol. xi, 1920; Edith K. Prideaux and G. R. Holt-Shafto, *Bosses and Corbels of Exeter Cathedral*, 1910; C. J. P. Cave, *Roof Bosses in Mediaeval Churches*, 1948, applies both to Exeter and Ottery. See also A. Gardner, *A Handbook of English Mediaeval Sculpture*, 1935, and *English Mediaeval Sculpture*, 1951.

For other aspects of ecclesiastical Exeter, see Beatrix F. Cresswell, *Exeter Churches*, 1908; Frances Rose-Troup, *Lost Chapels of Exeter*, 1908; Rev. J. F. Chanter, *The Custos and College of the Vicars Choral . . . of Exeter*, 1933; H. Lloyd Parry and Sir Harold Brakspear, *St. Nicholas' Priory, Exeter*, 1946.

For scholastic and economic affairs, see H. Lloyd Parry, *The Founding of Exeter School*, 1913; W. G. Hoskins, *Industry, Trade, and Population of Exeter*, 1935*; and H. Lloyd Parry, *The History of the Exeter Guildhall . . .*, 1936*. For the canal see my own article in *Country Life* of October 10th, 1952.

CREDITON

Polwhele is useful, see also R. J. King, *The Church . . . Crediton*, 1876; H. Michell Whitley, *Inventories of the Collegiate Churches of Crediton and Ottery*; Devonshire Association *Transactions*, 1902;

Rev. C. Felton-Smith, etc., *Records of the Church and Parish of Crediton*, 1909, 1925, 1928, and *Archaeological Journal*, 1913, pp. 527–9. See also (on St. Boniface), Rev. Dom. John Stephan, O.S.B., in Devonshire Association *Transactions*, 1951.

OTTERY ST. MARY

Exeter Diocesan Architectural Society, vol. i (1847), pp. 1–107; Lord Coleridge, *A History of the Town of Ottery St. Mary*, 1897; Rev. S. W. Cornish, *Short Notes on the Church and Parish of Ottery St. Mary*; Rev. F. B. Dickinson, *A Lecture on . . . the Church of St. Mary of Ottery*, 1897, 1906. The main work is Rev. J. N. Dalton, *The Collegiate Church of Ottery St. Mary*, 1917*. See also Frances Rose-Troup, *Bosses and Corbels in the Church of Ottery St. Mary*, 1922. See also H. Michell Whitley, *op. cit.*

TIVERTON

Martin Dunsford, *Historical Memoirs of the Town and Parish of Tiverton*, 1790*; J. Chaplin, *Picturesque Views of the River Exe*, 1819; Lt.-Col. William Harding, *History of Tiverton*, 1845 and 1847*; *The Stranger's Guide . . . for Tiverton*, 1855; F. J. Snell, *Chronicles of Twyford*, 1892; Rev. Edwin S. Chalk, *A History of the Church of St. Peter, Tiverton*, 1905*; F. J. Snell, *Blundells*, 1928. See also R. D. Blackmore, *Lorna Doone*.

CULLOMPTON

Devonshire Association *Transactions*, vol. xlii*, has important articles of the town's history and on the church.

TOPSHAM

Eric Delderfield, *The Raleigh Country*, 1950*, has useful material. See also Polwhele, Pevsner, and my own article in the *Devon County Journal*, Jan.–March 1951.

EXMOUTH

Rev. William Everitt, *Memorials of Exmouth*, 2nd edn., 1885*; Eric Delderfield, *op. cit.*, also applies. For A La Ronde, see pamphlet literature available at the house, also Christopher Hussey in *Country Life*, April 30th, 1938.

CONTENTS

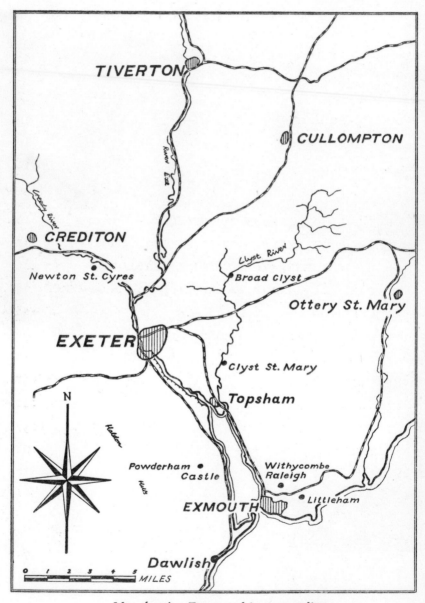

2　Map showing Exeter and its surroundings

3   Exeter: A Misericord in the Cathedral, *c.* 1260

4   Tiverton: On the Greenway Chapel, *c.* 1520

5   Ottery: A Capital, *c.* 1520

ELEPHANTS AND A SHIP

17

6   The Tomb of Bishop Edmund Stafford, *d.* 1419. (In the background
is that of Bishop Walter Bronescombe, *d.* 1280)

EXETER CATHEDRAL

Chapter I

THEIR HISTORY
PRE-REFORMATION

OUR Far West still begins at Exeter; the expresses, even the Cornish Riviera, no longer after Exeter have a schedule that makes them fully worthy of their title, a gentle access soon yields to the switchback ruggedness or tunnel-studded winding imposed by the wilder outlines of moor or cliff. When Nature brought the Exe and its tributaries to their lovely estuary through the fattest stretches of low-lying ground in Devon or Cornwall she made it certain that the river's lowest crossing-point would always be the site of a frontier town. Only in a distant future did Exeter become the capital of the whole peninsula that runs for another hundred miles before Cornwall's final Atlantic plunge. Our first view is that of a border city; that border character has persisted, the verdict of Nature being merely reaffirmed by the workings of modern transport.

Isca Dumnoniorum was the Roman name of the city. The *Isca* comes, as does the same prefix in *Isca Silurum*, now Caerleon-on-Usk, from the river that formed the barrier, here as in South Wales, between the fully settled lands of the Roman Empire and the Celtic territories beyond. The name seems certain to be Celtic, perhaps in essence the same as Axe, Esk, and Usk.* We have no sure knowledge of a Celtic settlement on the site. Nor does there seem to have been a very stirring career for Roman Exeter, in one a border fortress and a harbour (at the site of Topsham), the provincial centre of the Dumnonii who dwelt in the present Devon and Cornwall. Nor can we be sure that it continued as a human settlement when the Romans had gone. It seems that the district, never perhaps very thoroughly Romanised even as far west as Isca, was Celtic, Christian, and fairly peaceful before the Saxon occupiers got so far, and that the Saxons made the site of Exeter one of their final conquests.

* But see Sir Ifor Williams on pp. 5–6 of Lady Fox's *Roman Exeter*, 1952.

But in time "Exanceaster" became an outpost of Saxon Wessex. It was, perhaps, divided into a Celtic and a Saxon quarter, the Celts to the west, the Saxons to the east of a main street line running a little east of the present Fore Street as it plunges towards the river. A monastery was early established, and some of the churches may have Celtic origins or were founded by 700. But our chronicle is not of Exeter alone, and in these early Saxon years the greatest figure whose birth can be claimed by this East Devon district had probably been born in one of our other towns; in Crediton, whose name derives from the Creedy, an important tributary of the Exe.

St. Boniface, first named Winfred, lastingly famous as the Apostle of Germany, is said to have been born at Crediton, of good family, about 680. He did not long inhabit his birthplace; as a boy he early knew his vocation and went to nurture it in the monastery of Exeter, the abbot being Wulf hard, a man of saintly life who sent his pupil to the wider fields of work as a priest, missionary, and bishop that ended with Boniface's martyrdom in 755. Exeter may perhaps claim more credit for his lifework than Crediton itself. In any case Boniface remains the one saint, except the somewhat obscure local figure Sativola or Sidwell, whose connection with the city can be claimed. Not one of the bishops attained such a status, and despite a late mediaeval veneration for the uncanonised Bishops Berkeley (1327) and Lacy (1420–55) the Cathedral remained without its saintly relic or important pilgrimage shrine.

We know that Exeter was a fortified town, once taken by the enemy, and once besieged without success at the time of Alfred's Danish wars. Then under Athelstan it comes well into that process whereby the sway of Wessex and England was pushed west and made secure. We are told that the Celtic element was driven out and the town made a wholly English stronghold. The monastery was refounded as a community of Benedictines whose small church lay east of the present High Altar.

The Wessex diocese was divided when Bishop Asser of Sherborne died in 909. St. German's in Cornwall became a bishopric for over a century, for 141 years the Devon diocese had its seat at Crediton, now hallowed for its association with St. Boniface and so perhaps with a decisive advantage over the better sited Exeter. In 1003 Exeter was sacked by Sweyn and his invading Danes, but the tactical value of its steep ascent from the river crossing remained, and kept it as a fortified town, the natural centre both of power and communications in this richest part of the county. The ravages of robbers and pirates continued, the country round Exeter, Crediton included, was unsafe, in any case it became the general practice of the Western Church for bishops to be in the larger towns. Under Edward the Confessor, East Devon saw some of those changes, in land ownership as in church governance, that foreshadowed greater transformations after 1066.

Lyfing, bishop at the same time of Worcester, Crediton, and St. German's, died in 1046. Worcester was again given a separate bishop, but the spiritual oversight both of Devon and Cornwall was merged in the person of Leofric. He, in 1050, got Papal and Royal permission for the removal of his See from Crediton to the greater security of Exeter. The modest Saxon church of the Bene-dictines became the Cathedral, Edward the Confessor and his Queen Editha took part in a notable ceremony of installation, the Benedictines of St. Peter's, Exeter, went east to help man the Con-fessor's new abbey of St. Peter's at Westminster. The process was exactly what happened on a larger scale in Norman times when the bishops of village-cities had their cathedrals moved to towns of greater consequence—Elmham to Thetford and then Norwich, Dorchester to Lincoln, Selsey to Chichester, Wells to Bath. Crediton remained a small place, but the wealthy lordship of its manor stayed, along with many others, with the Bishops of Exeter all through the Middle Ages and till 1595, its church being of the dignity of a "collegiate" foundation of secular canons as was that of Exeter Cathedral itself.

A few years later East Devon saw a notable example of Edward's "Continental" policy in its more controversial phase. For the king gave the rich manor of Ottery to the Norman Cathedral Chapter of Rouen. The undoing of his gift was to be the prelude to the second most important act of church building that I have to notice in this book.

The Hastings battle did not at one stroke complete the conquest

of England. The fearful "harrying" of the Vale of York is a famous
incident; it is less well known that Exeter did not yield for nearly
two years. For William was delayed in his westward conquest;
the city of Exeter, and within it Gytha, the Danish widow of Earl
Godwin and the mother of Harold, stayed quietly unoccupied till
the spring of 1068. There followed a short siege, the flight abroad
of Gytha, the starting in the northern corner of the city, on a rocky
hillock of red sandstone, of the regularly fortified castle of Rougemont. Its custody, and the office of sheriff of Devon, went to a
relative of the Conqueror, Baldwin de Moeles or de Brionis; the
earldom of the county was given to his son. Baldwin was easily the
largest Devon landowner and almost its viceroy. In forty more years
the earldom had passed to his relative, Richard de Redvers (or
Rivers, *de ripariis*). By now the Redvers family held the large, rich
manor of Tiverton, so placed at the junction of the Exe and Lowman as to be dominant in the best stretch of level country north of
the district of Exeter, the key to the upper valley of the Exe and the
approaches of Exmoor. There, on a steep slope overhanging the
stream, as impregnable on its river side as Chepstow on its cliff, they
founded Tiverton Castle and made it their chief residence. Thus by
about 1120 came the full establishment of that feudal power which
was for centuries to be dominant in the Exe valley.

The Countess Gytha had richly endowed the church of St.
Olave in Exeter; her Danish birth may explain its dedication. The
Conqueror gave it to the Benedictines of Battle, the very foundation
that most clearly stood for the new political régime. About 1080 the
Battle monks (already in possession of the church revenues of
Cullompton) founded in the same district of the city the dependent
priory of St. Nicholas. It became a large enough foundation to
have its own conventual life, but it paid an annual sum to the
Sussex mother-house and the abbots of Battle appointed its
priors, in many cases from among their own Sussex monks. Four
priors of St. Nicholas' in their turn became abbots of Battle
and therefore members of the House of Lords. The revenues
of Cullompton Church were placed among the early possessions
of this Exeter priory.

Leofric died in 1072 and his successor in 1103. The next bishop was William Warelwast (1107–36), a nephew of the Conqueror, Norman, but with architectural tastes perhaps influenced by the church planning of Rhineland Romanesque. He started an entirely new cathedral, lying west of the Saxon one with open ground between the two. His building was less ambitious than the great abbeys or monastic cathedrals already started by the Normans or yet to be built. Yet we know that it had sturdy round pillars with scalloped capitals, and that the choir ended in an apse. More important, perhaps reminiscent of Rhineland practice, perhaps modelled on the plan of St. Osmund's Cathedral at Old Sarum, were the two massive flanking towers that are still the special features and glory of Exeter.

Other religious foundations followed in their turn—small monastic houses, hospitals, friaries. The city was also split into the many tiny parishes common in mediaeval English towns, the mayoralty and deanery both date from early in the thirteenth century. The castle was besieged and taken by Stephen at the beginning of the long civil war, but the city and the surrounding towns and villages stayed reasonably free to build up their civic and commercial life. Yet Exeter in time had much hindrance in the proper use of its river port.

Though the Romans had wisely, in view of the river's hydro-graphy, shipped to and from Topsham, the early mediaeval traders took small craft up to the city itself. But the Earls of Devon were hostile; it was one of many cases where enmity arose between a feudal lord and a growing bourgeois community. The Earls, with their lands down river from Exeter, and Powderham Castle to threaten the river approach, had the tactical advantage. It was an annoying practice of the times, specifically barred in Clause 33 of Magna Carta, for those who could do so to erect weirs across rivers needed by others for their fishing, mills, water supply, and naviga-tion. But Isabella de Fortibus, heiress of the Redvers family and widow of the Earl of Albemarle, became mistress of the Devon Earldom in 1262. In a little over twenty years she had provided for her own mills by blocking the Exe, about three miles down from Exeter, with the obstruction still known as Countess Weir; the modern Exeter by-pass goes over the river close at hand. The citizens got a verdict against her, and a narrow channel was cut through the middle, but in its essentials the blockage remained. At about the same time the Countess, being also Lady of Tiverton, indulged in more benevolent aquatic activity when she had a channel of fresh water, known as the Town Leat, taken into Tiverton from her lands to the north. It is thanks to her that runnels of clear water still run pleasantly through many of Tiverton's streets, and Wells and Cambridge are not the only towns with this prized, unusual amenity. Some forty years later the Courtenay heirs to the Devon title made a quay on their land at Topsham, and near it a tollhouse where dues were levied on Exeter's waterborne goods. This access by river was disputed throughout the Middle Ages between the earls and the city; nothing but the fall of the Courtenays (under Henry VIII's axe) and new advances in the cloth industry availed to give Exeter its due standing as a place of maritime commerce. At about the time of the early dispute we hear of Exmouth as a hamlet in the parish of Littleham. It was first a fishing place and a station for pilots in the estuary; by 1298 it was a small port, large enough then and later to contribute to the fleets required against Scotland and France.*

Late in the thirteenth century there started a series of builder-bishops who had the Cathedral transformed into the almost wholly Gothic church of today. The city itself became more and more the capital and social rendezvous of the two counties, with town houses of such nobles as the Courtenays and of the heads of large religious houses like Buckfast, Plympton, and Tavistock. Bishop Bronescombe (1257–80) was more than a building pioneer, for his diocesan record also puts him high among religious administrators. Then after 1300 the succession was caught up in the stormy politics of the time. For Bishop Stapledon (1308–26), a princely figure, founder of Exeter College, Oxford, and among Edward II's chief ministers, was left in charge of the capital when Edward retired before the invasion of his Queen Isabella and Mortimer her lover; he fell a victim to the murderous frenzy of the London mob. Bishop Berkeley only held the See for three months in 1327; it seems that,

* Its 10 ships and 193 men of 1346 may have included some from elsewhere in the Exe estuary.

though he had long been a canon of Exeter and was much respected, he owed his promotion to his coming of a family prominent among Edward's enemies. His successor was another of Exeter's many noble bishops, John de Grandisson (1327–69). His family had come from Grandson in what is now Switzerland; they married into a family related to Henry III's Queen and so settled in England and made a career as courtiers and as gentry in Herefordshire. The bishop's elder brother became Baron Grandisson and the bishop, wealthy and as princely in his outlook as Stapledon, held this temporal lordship as well as his spiritual peerage before he died. His Herefordshire connection had made him Mortimer's relative by marriage as well as his feudal client, so it was not politically surprising when the Pope at Avignon nominated him Bishop of Exeter. His luck outlasted his patron's fall in 1330, for Catherine his sister was wife to the William de Montacute who stood so close to the young Edward III when he seized political power, and who was actually given the delicate, dramatic task of bursting in on Isabella and Mortimer's adultery. As Countess of Salisbury, wife of a leading figure at the new Court, she could readily aid the bishop in his schemes of magnificence, particularly at Ottery.

By 1335 there had often been political trouble between England and France, and even before the Hundred Years' War the French churches that had land and dependant monasteries in England had found their possessions an awkward liability. In time they were to lose them all as "enemy property", but in a few cases the change was peacefully anticipated. So Grandisson, who had great devotion to Our Lady and wished to found a splendid church for her veneration, bought the manor and church presentation of Ottery from the Rouen canons in 1335 (negotiations had started the year before). There in 1337–8 he converted and enlarged an already fine church into a noble collegiate foundation with its head known as the Warden. Its régime, as also part of its architecture, was closely modelled on the bishop's cathedral of secular canons at Exeter; the statutes themselves seem to have been a model for the even more famous royal collegiate foundations soon set up at St. George's, Windsor, and at St. Stephen's, Westminster, whose chapel was long to serve as the House of Commons. The main work at

Ottery was swiftly accomplished; the profusion of Grandisson and Montacute heraldry makes it seem certain that the bishop and his sister spent liberally on the scheme.

Grandisson also nearly completed the long refashioning of his cathedral; the final touches to the main work came under Branting-ham (1370–94). Of the fifteenth-century bishops, Edmund Lacy (1420–55) was venerated for his piety and was a fit host for Henry VI in 1452. George Neville (1458–65) owed his early bishopric, when only twenty-four, to his being the Kingmaker's brother. He went later to the Archbishopric of York, and there his politics caused his ruin and disgrace. The city of Exeter saw something of the Wars of the Roses, for there was a short seige during the King-maker's rebellion in 1470 and it was from there that Warwick fled to France. The Courtenays were strong Lancastrians, and Exeter was twice again a base for their party—for Warwick on his last return to England, and in 1471 for the adherents of Margaret of Anjou while they gathered the western army that was defeated at Tewkesbury. In 1483 there was the visit to Exeter of Richard III, and the incident told by Shakespeare* where the confusion of sounds between Rougemont and Richmond is said to have struck fear into Richard's heart. In the meantime the city's civic standing and commerce were slowly growing despite weirs and Courtenays. With the cloth trade now well established as a west-country industry we come, in 1490, to the incorporation of the Guild of Weavers, Fullers, and Shearmen. Yet Exeter's growth as a lay community was still modest, and the Poll Tax figures of 1377, revealing a population that probably stood between 2,500 and 3,000, showed it no more than twenty-third in order of population among the boroughs of England. Politics of the stormier kind, and also civil wars, were still important, never more so than in the year 1497.

It was a year of two rebellions against the Tudor Government of Henry VII. The Cornish insurgents of the early summer passed round to the north of Exeter on their march to Blackheath and defeat. But the army of Perkin Warbeck, likewise starting in Cornwall and getting no nearer to London than the area of

* Richard III, Act IV, Sc. 2.

Taunton, made a direct attack on Exeter, on September 17th and 18th; the Earl of Devon commanded the defence. The Cornish forced the North Gate (in the middle of what is now an area of rebuilding after the more destructive assaults of 1942) and got some distance into the city towards Rougemont. But they were driven out and went away, discouraged, by way of Cullompton to Taunton; their failure may have been as decisive, psychologically speaking, as Monmouth's turning away from Bristol in 1685. The King was in Exeter for a month in the autumn to do clement justice and pacify his disturbed far-western province. In another four years his foreign policy touched Exeter in another way. For the girl princess, Catherine of Aragon, stayed in the Deanery on her way from Plymouth to her first marriage, with Prince Arthur, that ended so soon with death at Ludlow and the magnificent obsequies at Worcester. The noisy weathercock on St. Mary Major's tower disturbed her sleep, so it was dismantled to relieve her. A quaint little annoyance; she was to have worse in England to worry her as years wore on.

The pre-Reformation phase ends with another series of courtier bishops. Fox (1487–91) and Oliver King (1492–5) were non-resident and more famous in later appointments. Hugh Oldham (1504–19) was a Mancunian, a friend of Lady Margaret Beaufort and distinguished not only as a zealous diocesan but as a patron of learning at Oxford and in his home town. John Veysey (1519–51 and again 1553–4) had been dean before he became bishop. He was tutor to Princess Mary and often had commitments and interests to keep him away from the west.* The city, and with it the bulk of Devon and Cornwall, remained mainly Catholic in feeling. There was also by now a new growth in the making of woollen cloth that was to be the economic mainstay of East Devon. We hear that the only market for wool, yarn, and kersies in Devon was once at Crediton, but Exeter got one established in 1538. In the meantime a leading figure in this great activity of the rising bourgeois class was John Greenway of Tiverton.

So much weaving was done at Tiverton that local wool was not enough. So Greenway imported it, sold it to the weavers, and then

* A brilliant pen portrait of him is in A. L. Rowse's *Tudor Cornwall*.

exported the cloth; he was typically an early capitalist and his chapel makes it clear how much store he set by shipping. He dominated the economic life of Tiverton, became the main rebuilder of the church and the town's chief benefactor till Peter Blundell later surpassed him. His opposite numbers at Exeter, like him in some cases Merchant Adventurers of London and incorporating the Exeter Company in 1556, seem to have made less of a mark, and John Lane of Cullompton did more in his noble church to emulate Greenway.

A contemporary in Tiverton was splendid after an older manner. She was the Lady Catherine Courtenay, a dowager countess and a princess as well, for she was the youngest daughter of Edward IV and so the aunt of Henry VIII. Her husband, William Courtenay, Earl of Devon, had died in 1511; she lived on for sixteen years, kept lordly state in Tiverton Castle, and died in November 1527. There followed a funeral that must have been Tiverton and East Devon's last, most gorgeous farewell to the old order of feudal pomp. Norroy King at Arms and Richmond Herald came specially from London to conduct the ceremonies, the church was hung in black and lit with 800 tapers; a great concourse of clergy and gentry were there to honour the princess. There were three High Masses; of Our Lady, of the Trinity, and of Requiem, the Abbots of Torre and Ford being present; and above them the Prior of Montacute, Thomas Chard, who had been Warden of Ottery and was a titular bishop *in partibus*, his duties being to assist in Exeter and Bath and Wells dioceses.* A sumptuous dinner followed the tiring ceremonies; there was never a hint of the coming Reformation nor yet of the Courtenays' collapse.

But both events were under way in a dozen years. The smaller religious houses were suppressed in 1536, the two Exeter friaries within two years more. Some women made a violent demonstration when the Commissioners were in Exeter and their servant was pulling down the rood-loft in the nave of St. Nicholas' priory. But the work proceeded, and then in 1538 came the royal blow at the Courtenays.

* The Abbot of Ford was another Thomas Chard. See Somerset Archaeological Society Transactions, vols. 37, 42, 74.

The son of the late Lady Catherine was Henry, not only Earl of Devon but also made Marquis of Exeter by his cousin Henry VIII. He long flourished in magnificence as one of the greatest nobles in the realm. But in time he came into danger by reason of that very nearness to the throne, for he, like Henry VIII, was grandson to Edward IV. It seems also that his retinue unwisely paraded their master's position, and there may have been some tactical unwisdom on the Marquis' part. In 1538 he was attainted and put to death in London. Next year an Act was passed which enabled Exeter city to deal with the weirs and clear the way for navigation. Work started about 1544, but time proved the need for more drastic and artificial measures.

For a few years the colleges and chantries survived the monasteries and friaries, but the dissolution of nearly all colleges came in 1545, and Crediton and Ottery then closed their long, uneventful career of ordered liturgical observance. The Ottery manor went to the future Protector Somerset and much of the church revenue to St. George's, Windsor. For the two churches, now parochial, a very similar organisation was worked out, the one being probably adapted from the other. Each church was to be maintained by a body of "Governors", twelve at Crediton, at Ottery four with eight "Assistant Governors" to help them from 1552.

But religious changes, accompanied as they were with much social distress of a kind that helped to make many areas of England turbulent in 1549, did not go smoothly in the west. The climax came in the widespread rebellion (not only in Devon and Cornwall) against the New Prayer Book of 1549; the English Service that replaced the Latin Mass was called a "Christmas game" in the rebels' statement of policy. The chief scenes of struggle were East Anglia and the west; never before or later was Exeter so much the centre of a national crisis.

The rising started and ended at Sampford Courtenay in mid-Devon; the tract of country between the moors was a main gathering ground for the insurgent forces. Edward VI's cause was chiefly upheld (not very successfully till the royal army arrived) by the landowners who had done well from the great parcelling out of church property—Carews, Dennises, Raleighs, Grenvilles, most notably by

John, Lord Russell, later Earl of Bedford and commander of the troops who came west to quell the rising. The first attack on the rebels was while they were at Crediton and advancing on Exeter and the east country beyond its river. They had blocked the road and fortified some thatched barns on either side. The attackers, quite lawfully on any military consideration, fired the barns and forced a way into the town. But the burning was interpreted against them, and "Crediton Barns" became a social slogan to set beside the clamour for a restored Mass and the banner of the Five Wounds.

Exeter, despite many Catholic sympathisers within, was firmly held for the Crown, confirming its tradition of SEMPER FIDELIS. But the ground west of the Exe fell easily to the rebels; the parish priest of St. Thomas, one Robert Welsh, being among their leaders, one can imagine his church as their chief place of worship in the coming siege.

The city was beleaguered from early July to the first week in August. The main operations were farther east as the rebel forces tried to bar the way to the relieving army with its detachment of Flemish mercenaries. But there were skirmishings round Exeter itself, and much hunger within, while the rebels tried to undermine the walls and fire the gates. They would also have burnt the city with red-hot shot had not Welsh restrained the gunners.

The chief battles were in the country between Exeter and Ottery, and notably in the valley of the Clyst that joins the Exe estuary at Topsham. The first skirmish was at Fenny Bridges, a multiple crossing* of the Otter a little up-river from Ottery on the Exeter–Honiton road. Then came the forcing of the rebels' base at Clyst St. Mary, finally, on August 5th, a hard fight and heavy slaughter as Russell and his royal troops severely beat the besieging rebels on Clyst Heath where Exeter's outskirts now spread eastward with modern housing estates. The city was relieved next day, the pursuit going westward towards Cornwall and ending with a battle at Sampford Courtenay. At Exeter there were executions to follow the deaths by battle. Most notable was the hanging, in Mass vestments

---

* Leland says of the river, that it was "devided into four armes by pollicy to serve grist and tukking milles".

and from his own church tower, of the vicar of St. Thomas', a grim, conspicuous proof that Reformation was now ascendant. In 1551 Miles Coverdale the Reformer became Bishop of Exeter for two years till Mary deprived him (he was not for the burning) and restored Veysey her old tutor to his See.

Chapter II

THEIR HISTORY
THE NEXT THREE CENTURIES

SINCE the Reformation our story is more of tendencies than of major incidents; only the Civil War, 1688, and 1772 stand strongly out in the sequence of historic events or literary association. The Bishops of Exeter, reduced in income and less lordly in living, were not so conspicuous as in the days of a Grandisson or a Stafford, the nobility were less dominant over the life of the towns, though Exmouth was to owe much to noble enterprise in its growth as a resort. But Exeter still had the town houses of the gentry—of Bedfords, Bampfyldes, and their like—to replace those of abbots and priors and to make of the city the social capital of its province. Underlying the whole we find the intensive development, throughout our area, of the cloth trade as East Devon's mainstay; it made an economic unit of the whole Exe basin from Cullompton to Crediton, from Tiverton through Exeter as its nodal point to the shipping in the estuary and outside Exmouth.

The cloth trade was not new to Devon in the mid-Tudor decades, but it was after about 1550 that it gained great impetus, the more so as there grew up the export links with the Netherlands and Central Europe. East Devon, along with the border country of Somerset and Wiltshire, south Gloucestershire, East Anglia, and the north, became one of the greatest textile areas of England. For two and a half centuries the industry persisted in greater or less prosperity, with its final decline not till after the Napoleonic War.

At Exeter we soon hear of more effective steps than river improvement to attract navigation right up to the city. In 1563-4 work started on that historic waterway, the Exeter Canal. It was a short, shallow channel, leading no farther down river than Countess Weir and only usable by small barges so that seaborne commerce had to tranship at Topsham. The engineer called in was a Welshman, John Trew of Glamorgan, but the main novelty of his work may

7   Exeter: Southernhay Baths, by Lethbridge, 1821
From "Devonshire Illustrated", 1830

8   Tiverton: The Market Cross, *c.* 1732 (pulled down in 1783)
From Lt.-Col. Harding, "The History of Tiverton", 1845

BUILDINGS NOW DESTROYED

9 Exeter: The Quay and Warehouses (early nineteenth century)

10 Crediton: In the Market, *c.* 1820

COMMERCE

have owed its inspiration to the trading contact with the Netherlands that was already developing. For the canal had three pound-
locks of a type already familiar to the Dutch. Its historic importance
also comes from its being the first of our canals. The canal was
improved about 1675–80, and then, as we shall see, was twice
lengthened and made deeper, onwards from 1698 and in the 1820's.

Such aids to navigation were bound to help both Exeter (whose
people may have numbered 7,500 in the middle of Elizabeth I's reign)
and the other clothing towns. The second most important centre,
at times almost equal to Exeter and more exclusively concerned with
cloth, was Tiverton. In both places the areas towards the Exe were
given over to the industry, the low-lying districts became subdivided with leats to bring running water to the fulling mills, the
meadows were crossed over, as old maps show, by the tenter-racks
for stretching and drying the finished cloth.* Then when the time
came for large-scale finishing mills it was in these same areas, at
Tiverton and Ottery, that the factories, with their need for water
power, were built. The towns had their varying specialities;
Crediton became famous for the fineness of its spinning, Tiverton
for its coarser kersies and later for worsteds and damasks. The one
constant cause of interruption, in the outlying towns with their
excessive use of cob and thatch, came with the devastating fires
which often burnt houses in their hundreds and so, in this period of
domestic weaving, caused serious trading loss. Tiverton was fear-
fully ravaged in 1598, 1612, and 1731, with lesser fires in 1625,
1661, and 1785. Crediton was badly damaged in 1743 and on a
smaller scale in 1766, 1769, and 1772. Ottery had fires in 1604 and
1767, and lastly a bad one as late as 1866. At Cullompton there
were fires in 1682 and 1798, but the chief conflagration was in 1839,
There were also plagues at times, and frequent riots when workers,
having no electoral outlet or machinery for the peaceful discussion
of their problems, made serious tumults when seeking to remedy
economic and political grievances. Tiverton in particular was
prone to the trouble, but Exeter was not immune. The worst phase
of the riots was nearly always preceded by vast draughts of the cider
whose making, particularly round Crediton, was a leading local

* See Celia Fiennes' excellent description of Exeter.

pursuit. Feminine influences, too, were at work, notably in the riot at Tiverton when the women were those who pulled off the mayor's wig and tweaked his nose. But trade continued, and Tiverton saw the reverse side of rioting when the town's decline was arrested by the coming of a new trade hounded out of the Midlands by Luddite frenzy. The last link in the chain was still in large measure the port of Topsham, of use for the bringing in of foreign wool and Dutch linen, and for the shipping out of Devon cloth.

But trade apart, mid-Tudor Exeter had also its connection with men whose fame lies in other fields. Sir Thomas Bodley, founder of the Bodleian, was born in Exeter in 1544. He did not maintain much connection with his native city, but his brother Lawrence was a canon of Exeter and a benefactor both to the city and, by means of books lifted from the Cathedral Library, to his brother's Oxford foundation. About 1547 the city was the birthplace of Nicholas, son of Richard Hilliard, a rich jeweller and goldsmith; the boy followed his father's trade, but is best known as one of our greatest practitioners of another precise art, that of the painter of miniatures.

The main Tudor names in East Devon clothing, famous also for their charities, are those of Waldron and Blundell. John Waldron of Tiverton was born about 1520, made a fortune, and in his life-time laid out money on the Almshouses in Westexe that bear his name. Peter Blundell is yet more renowned. He, too, was Tiverton born in about 1520, but lived till 1601. His business interests as a clothier were vast, lying both in Tiverton and in London, where he died. But, along with Exeter, his native town was the main receiver of his bounty. He was a bachelor, and had the more to spend, but much went also to relatives, and his nephews made Blundell generosity a family tradition. For George Slee was the founder of an almshouse, while another nephew by marriage, Robert Comyn (alias Chilcot), who was also Blundell's chief clerk, more closely imitated his uncle by starting a free school for the elementary educa-tion of the boys who were to proceed to Peter Blundell's own foundation.

Blundell's has far outgrown any local fame; from an early stage it took boarders from afar and so spread its reputation away from Devon. So Blackmore's John Ridd in *Lorna Doone* is true enough to the facts of 1673, though I am told that this picture of life in the old Blundell's is nearer to the conditions round 1840 when the future author was a pupil. It became an easy transition from local grammar school to one of national standing; in any case the process was aided by the fame of such old boys as Blackmore himself and of Frederick Temple, in time to be Bishop of Exeter (1869–85) and later the first of his name to attain Canterbury. The school's foundation, as given in Blundell's will of 1599, was lavish; it was for a master, an usher, and 150 boys, with three scholarships each at Balliol, Oxford, and the newly founded Sidney Sussex at Cambridge. The plan's achievement was supervised by a man important in the Law and the financing of enterprise overseas, Lord Chief Justice Popham of Wellington, Somerset, who died in 1607, three years after the building was finished on its floodprone site by the Lowman. There till the 1880's the school continued; the most famous name among its masters (1734–9) was Samuel Wesley, the elder brother of John and Charles.

In Exeter an important school was started in the first third of the seventeenth century. The ancient buildings of St. John's Hospital had been used before the Reformation for the boarding of boys at a high school which continued, without making permanent use of the St. John's premises, till the middle of the eighteenth century. Then in the 1620's the hospital buildings became a children's workhouse, the task being pinmaking which was an occupation also found suitable for similarly placed children in Bristol and Gloucester. Then in 1629 Alderman Thomas Walker left money for the foundation, by the city, of a grammar school which used part of St. John's and was in operation by 1634, the old chancel of the hospital church being fitted as its chapel and tuition taking place in the upper part of a horizontally divided nave. In another three years a Free English School was also at work within the hospital premises, while the ground floor of the transformed nave was profitably let off as a wool hall to serve the purchasing needs of Exeter's allimportant cloth trade.

We may suppose that the trading element of East Devon was generally sympathetic to Parliament in the Civil War. But the clothiers were not strong enough, as were their fellow clothiers at

Taunton and the seamen of Plymouth, to secure the towns for their cause.*

At first, in 1642, both Exeter and Tiverton declared for Parlia/ment, with most of Devon held on the same behalf; the Parliamen/tarian Earl of Bedford had influence enough in the capital to sway the position. For a time the city was active as a fortified Parliament base, but things changed after Lord Stamford, the Governor, had sallied towards hostile Cornwall and had lost the battle of Stratton. Tiverton fell to the Royalists in August 1643, and Exeter sur/rendered next month to Prince Maurice and Sir John Berkeley; an effort to relieve it by sea had failed when guns on shore played on the Earl of Warwick's incoming ships. Berkeley was made Governor, and under him the city was so secure that Queen Henrietta Maria came there for her delivery in the summer of 1644. She lodged in Bedford House, and there on June 16th gave birth to the Princess Henrietta. In a few days more she left, the baby remaining at Exeter till she was nearly two. For Lord Essex was approaching, and indeed for a few days held Tiverton, on his disastrous foray into the Royalist west. In a few days more the King was at Exeter in pursuit.

The operations of 1645 and 1646 were in two phases, being part of the final campaigning after Charles' decisive defeat in the field at Naseby. The last considerable royal army had been confined in Devon and Cornwall; early in the autumn of 1645 the pursuit began; Cullompton fell to Parliament on October 15th. On October 18th and 19th Fairfax and Massey took Tiverton and its castle. Fairfax then moved to Ottery; for six weeks till early December his headquarters were there while he sent to occupy Crediton and had Cromwell with him to plan the next moves. All winter Exeter was ever more closely blockaded; the royal army was beaten at Torrington in February 1646, and its remnants later surrendered in Cornwall. The last moves were concerned with Exeter itself. The Royalists had built a fort at Exmouth to command the river entrance, but this fell in mid/March and the city, after a short siege, on April 13th. Princess Henrietta was allowed to leave

* See Jack Simmons, on Exeter in the Civil War, in *Parish and Empire*, 1952, pp. 88–96.

for France, there to become the Duchess of Orleans; she died, sadly and young, in 1670.

The events of 1688 come as a political aftermath to the Civil War; Exeter's part in the early days of the Glorious Revolution was vital yet is not widely known.

William of Orange had landed at Brixham on November 5th; he advanced with caution on Exeter and his first envoy was kept in custody, for the mayor and nearly all the council were of Jacobite sympathies. But William's artillery and heavy stores were disembarked, not in Torbay but at Topsham and so by land carriage to Exeter when William had gained possession. He made a splendid entry on November 9th, but the political atmosphere was still chilly; it is even said that his natural caution made him consider withdrawal. He stayed twelve days in Exeter which had been his first capture among English cities; only at the end of that period had he rallied enough support, both locally and from nearer the Court, to venture from his first important holding to the later stages of his triumphant advance.

The East Devon clothiers gained greatly from William's economic policy. For the coming years brought the vast increase in their trade with William's Netherlands, and so through Rotterdam (or through Hamburg and Bremen) to the Central European markets that made the early eighteenth century the peak period of East Devon textiles. There was the improvement, perhaps with Dutch technical assistance, of the canal, a Dutch colony of factors at Topsham, and strong Dutch influences on local building. There were technical changes, from kersies to worsteds at Tiverton, and then to damasks, the coming of such German immigrants as the Duntzes and Barings. These foreigners indeed became a mainstay of the trade when conditions called for a change from domestic to factory weaving. Not only were the Barings, of Bremen and then of Exeter, the founders of a renowned financial house, they were also, especially at Tiverton in 1765, the capitalists to whom the weavers turned for new enterprise and the maintenance of trade. For by the later years of the eighteenth century the industry was past its peak and feeling the pressure of northern competition; the opening years of the French Revolutionary War saw the loss of foreign markets, and the high demand of the Napoleonic War served only to arrest decline and not to increase the total of business done. A last effort, with the capital of the Yonges and Duntzes behind it (Sir John Duntze being by now a leading local figure, a banker, and long an M.P. for Tiverton) was made when a great cloth factory was built at Ottery; another soon followed at Tiverton, at first for cotton and then for woollens. But the Ottery factory was on silk within a few years, and at Tiverton the mill closed (some of its workers moving to a mill built at Cullompton) with the end of war contracts; what saved the town was the coming, in 1816, of John Heathcoat whose patent for the making by machinery of bobbin lace had been frustrated by the Luddites of the Midlands (their attack on his works was known as "the Loughborough job"). So started the famous firm of silk and lace net manufacturers that has ever since been the chief economic feature of Tiverton. By 1834 they had over 800 at work in the factory and some 1,500 outworkers, and the Factory Commissioners who visited Tiverton that year could say that "nothing we have yet met with has been equal to this great establishment"; their whole report on its working conditions was high praise. But weaving is no more at Crediton, Cullompton, Exeter, or Ottery, and Topsham had to switch, in the nineteenth century, to the building and repair of sailing vessels, and to the general activity of a minor, slowly declining coastal port. But at Exmouth there was an advance in matters maritime when the dock for coasting vessels was opened in 1865.

There are also continuing associations with literature and art.

Another brilliant miniaturist came from East Devon when Richard Cosway, son of a master at Blundell's, was born at Tiverton in 1742. His career was to lie among Court and fashionable circles in London, in particular in the entourage of "Prinny", but he was not unmindful of his native town, and in 1784 gave the church his altar painting of St. Peter escaping from prison; like most of his earlier paintings it is a large-scale work, not a miniature, and is still in the building.

In 1760 Rev. John Coleridge became vicar of Ottery, and there, on October 21st, 1772, his youngest son, Samuel Taylor Coleridge, was born. The family had come from near Crediton, and the boy spent much time with relatives there as well as in Ottery. His birth-place, too, was an important influence on his early life, and it was at Ottery that there occurred the famous incident when the boy was lost and out all night by the river. Even had the connection been slighter than it was, one could be sure of Ottery's claim, St. Boniface perhaps excluded, to the most important figure whose birth is recorded in this book. Then in the following century East Devon had more than a passing importance for Thackeray's early life. For his home for a time was at Larkbeare House near Whimple, Ottery being the "Clavering St. Mary" and Exeter the "Chatteris" of *Pendennis*. Then when we turn to politics and the Law we find Coleridge's nephew, John Taylor Coleridge, and that John Taylor's son, the first Lord Coleridge, achieving eminence respec-tively as a judge and Lord Chief Justice. Palmerston, being an Irish peer and so able to sit in the Commons, was a Member, for thirty years from 1835, for Tiverton. Downes House at Crediton was by now the home of the Bullers, and there, in 1839, the future General Sir Redvers Buller was born; he died at his birthplace in 1908.

Georgian Exeter had maintained its place as a provincial capital; its domestic architecture was worthy of its social pre-eminence. By the Regency period the city and its surroundings "within four miles northward" also became a villa-studded district of genteel residence and elegant retirement; one would like to be able to identify the Barton Cottage chosen for their retreat by Mrs. Dashwood and her daughters. It is consistent with the surviving Exeter villas that it was regular, devoid of thatch and honeysuckle and so, to para-phrase Jane Austen, "defective as a cottage".

Though *Sense and Sensibility* makes mention of Dawlish, we are more concerned with the growth as a seaside resort of Exmouth, frequented not only by Exeter citizens, but also by persons of less provincial fame.

The process is said to have started about 1720, a judge on circuit having become unwell and then being restored by a visit to the village, still a small place with its church an ill-served chapel of ease to Littleham. Visitors of quality came as the century wore on. Lady Glenorchy, the friend and collaborator of the Countess of

Huntingdon, was there in 1776 and founded the Glenorchy Congregational Chapel in 1777; by contrast another famous lady, Mrs. Thrale, was a visitor about 1788. Development was soon well under way, its sponsorship coming largely from the Lords Rolle whose family had succeeded the Dennises at Bicton. By about 1820 there were Assembly Rooms, a theatre, a new Holy Trinity chapel, and an elegant blend of local and more distant visitors. The town became the residence, for much of a critical, financially unedifying period in their relationship, of the Duke of York's notorious mistress, Mary Anne Clarke. Lady Nelson was often there from 1816; when she died in London in 1831, it was at Littleham that her burial took place. Lady Byron was also an Exmouth visitor, and Holy Trinity provided his first post as an organist to the young Samuel Sebastian Wesley. The coastline at Exmouth is also notable for the beauty of its evening skies as the sun goes down over the estuary or towards Torbay. So Exmouth was for twenty years the residence, till his death in 1861, of the important landscape artist Francis Danby.

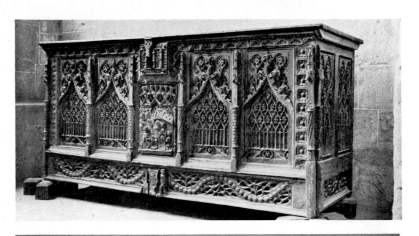

11 Crediton: The Church Chest

12 Exeter: St. Petrock's (originally in St. Kerrian's). Last Judgment by Weston, from Ivie Monument, *c.* 1717

13 Exeter: St. Mary Steps. The Norman Font, with its late Gothic Cover

14　Exeter: The Cathedral Choir

Chapter III

EXETER
CITY, COUNTY TOWN, CATHEDRAL

THERE is little in modern Exeter to see of the Roman *Isca Dumnoniorum*. Traces of walling have indeed shown that the mediaeval fortifications in part coincided with their Roman predecessors, there have been varied finds of loose objects, and since the Second World War the opening out of previously built-up spaces has made it possible to find remains of wooden-framed houses perhaps as early as A.D. 55–75. There were also baths; they had a central plunge on a smaller scale, like the better preserved swimming pool at Bath. But the Roman city with its later forum and houses in time was thoroughly destroyed and overlaid; we do not even have a mediaeval street plan that seems to correspond to the Roman lay-out. Moreover, the Saxon city, all but some walling of the small church of St. George near South Street, and more foundations below the Lady Chapel of the Cathedral, has also passed away. For our main purposes the architecture of Exeter begins with the Normans.

Our survey starts, as I prefer that it should do even in a city where the Cathedral is overwhelmingly the main building, with the habitations of the temporal power. At the northern corner of the city (which lies aslant the compass points so that the "North" Gate was really north-west, and the "East" Gate north-east) the Conqueror and Sheriff Baldwin built Rougemont Castle, its inner fortress being on the red, elevated rock that marked the summit of the hill which rises above the ridge as it slopes to the Exe. Very little remains of what they or any mediaeval successors built within the surviving, partly later, circuit of the outer walls. The one convincing reminder of Norman origins is the main gateway, its arch flanked by shafts which have the simple cushion capitals of about 1080. But otherwise the castle buildings are largely Georgian. Rougemont, though a royal castle and then for some centuries part of the Duchy of Cornwall estates, was not before the mid-nineteenth century within the City of Exeter, and belonged to the County of Devon. Assizes were therefore held within its walls (though we twice hear of Blundell's at Tiverton being used when there was plague at Exeter), and by 1773 the courts seemed inconvenient and unworthy of their purpose. "Improvements" were set afoot whereby the ancient fortress was turned into the pleasant semblance of an eighteenth-century park, and so it remains, with trees, walks, and delightful views as one strolls within the castle or beyond its walls in the elevated gardens of Northernhay. The main new building was the Shire Hall, a severe, unadorned, yet well proportioned block with an arched and pedimented stone façade; its was started in 1774, the builders being Philip Stowey and Thomas Jones.

There is much to see of the circuit of Exeter's mediaeval walls. As in some other cities, the goodness of their preservation was un-suspected till bombs removed an overlaying of more recent buildings. But round much of the city, particularly on its eastern side toward Southernhay and along the walks that overlook the valley which shielded Exeter on the north-west, there are many stretches of the red sandstone walls with their rounded mediaeval bastions. The gates have been more unlucky, for not one outlasted the pullings down of the eighteenth century. The old prints reveal our sad loss, particu-larly in the "East" and "South" gates with their great rounded towers to flank the roadways.

I find it hard to believe that Exeter never had a bridge before the thirteenth century, but our first record concerns one built in 1257 by Mayor Walter Gervis. It had an approaching causeway (which still survives), piers of stone, and an upper structure of wood. There were later alterations, and Leland speaks of fourteen arches (pre-sumably he reckons in the causeway). The bridge of the Middle Ages was a little downstream from the line of New Bridge Street and the present erection. This in its turn replaces a Georgian bridge whose beginnings were unhappy. Started in 1770 to the designs of one Dixon of London, it soon collapsed and had to be rebuilt by John Goodwin of Exeter. The arches and balustrades over the leats and alleys of Exe Island are surviving relics of this completer eighteenth-century work.

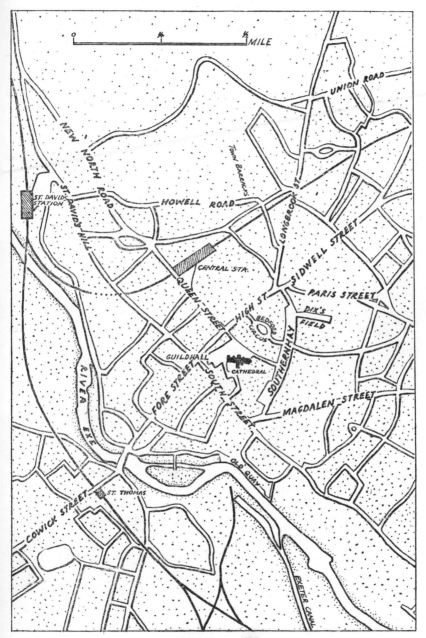

15 Street Plan of Exeter

Up in the main city, High Street is still dominated by the later portions of the Guildhall, of all Exeter buildings the most familiar after the Cathedral. But the work which we see from the street, being late Elizabethan, is far junior to the oblong building which runs back from the street and whose eastern end is masked by the projecting portico, and by its dignified upper room which is now the Mayor's parlour and succeeds a late mediaeval Guild Chapel of St. George.

Exeter had a Guildhall by about 1160; this hall in its turn was rebuilt about 1330. There may be some fourteenth-century masonry in the walls, but in its main structure, and notably in the timbers of its arch-braced and delicately ornamented roof, the hall dates from about 1470; it may have been to honour the "Kingmaker" that the brackets were adorned with his Warwick bear and ragged staff. There had long been some kind of sheltering penthouse or portico in front of the hall, and below its eastern end some readily available cellar space for the keeping of prisoners. Now in the fifteenth century it became a custom, and one long maintained, that stalls and a town pump should be placed before the Guildhall. Then in the next century the pavement and stalls got better shelter by the building of the feature so famous today. The group consisting of the portico and the rooms above, with their main colonnade, Corinthian pillarets, and mullioned windows, is a typically hybrid, Elizabethan-Renaissance work (16). It was put up in 1592–4 and is much worn from the poor durability of the Beer stone. We may date the wooden door from the same era, as also the interior features now seen in the hall. For the richly carved panelling, now picked out with the heraldry of the Exeter companies and of many past mayors, is also Elizabethan of the period when the city was recovering from Reformation turmoils and gladly witnessing the rapid rise of her trade in cloth. There have been many modern changes, with galleries altered or pulled down, but the fine brass chandelier, of 1789 and by John Pike of Bridgwater, is still there as a noble embellishment.

A short glance is enough for all other buildings but one of Exeter's "County Town" architecture. The Shire Hall we have seen, the asylum need not detain us, the late eighteenth-century

16 Exeter: The Guildhall Front, 1592–4

17　Exeter: The Monument to Edward Cotton (d. 1675), Treasurer,
in the Cathedral

STUART DIVINE

prison, a building that included the improvements advocated by Howard, was replaced, on its fine site on Danes' Hill, by another dignified brick building now a century old; the gateway of the 1790's was, however, allowed to remain. Off the Topsham road the barracks are late Georgian in red brick; they were started in 1804 and a pediment contains a large achievement of the Royal Arms of George III. The original workhouse, finished in 1707, had a three-sided court and in its own time was reckoned the finest work-house in England. A more notable, and surviving Georgian achievement is the Devon and Exeter Hospital.

It was one of many such infirmaries started in provincial cities during the middle decades of the eighteenth century. The year 1729, and the whole decade of the 1730's, had been a bad period for Exeter's health. A body of citizens, headed by Dean Clarke, who had already done much to found the infirmary at Winchester, made plans, from the summer onwards in 1741 (itself a bad year of epidemic typhus both in Exeter and Tiverton) for a new hospital. John Tuckfield, one of Exeter's M.P.s, gave land in Southernhay, the foundation stone was laid on August 27th, and the first patients went there in 1743. There have been many additions, but the bulk of the first building survives as the centre of the present hospital, an excellent, pedimented mid-Georgian building in red brick having some inner rooms adorned with panelling and architectural decoration in Roman Doric. In another eighty years Southernhay, by then a delightful residential promenade, was embellished by the Grecian portico, with square piers and Attic decoration, of a suite of baths. They were opened in 1821, the architect being Lethbridge of Exeter. Unhappily they did not long prosper, and their demolition was a genuine architectural loss.

The Cathedral was served in the Middle Ages by a Chapter of secular canons with the officers usual in such a body—dean, precentor, chancellor, and treasurer (each office with its own arms), and below them by the Vicars Choral who resided to take the places (*vices*) of absent and non-resident canons. The buildings ancillary to the Cathedral, not all of them physically linked to the

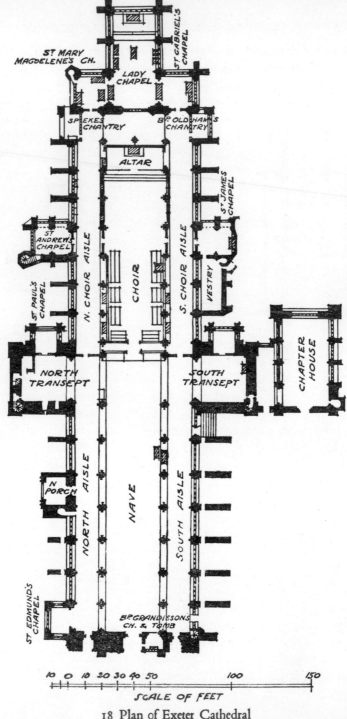

SCALE OF FEET

18 Plan of Exeter Cathedral

church and cloisters as in a monastic cathedral like Canterbury, but often cast loosely round the fringes of the Close, appeared, and to some extent were, haphazard in their grouping, though readily intelligible in their functions. But the church, proceeding through

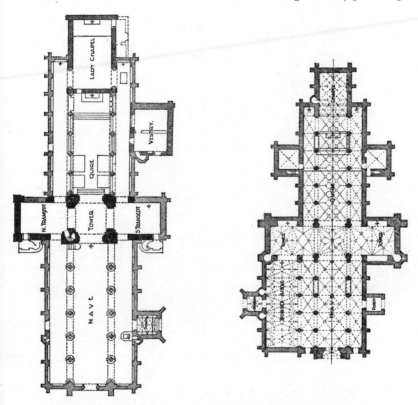

19, 20 Plan of Crediton (*left*) and of Ottery St. Mary Minsters, drawn to the same scale as the plan of Exeter Cathedral (*opposite*)

many stages of plan and reconstruction, was as regular and orderly as any in England.

At a first glance the two splendid towers alone are Norman, but the design of William Warelwast's church conditioned the altered Cathedral of the later Middle Ages, and much Norman masonry, along with some twelfth-century features, is in the present fabric. The aisle walls of the nave, with shallow pilasters still visible behind the buttresses that stand clear to reveal them, are Norman work. The second Cathedral was about 240 feet long, flanked by the massive arcaded towers(22) but without open transepts of the usual type; it seems that the arcades were continuous from the nave to the short apsidal choir, thus setting the precedent of a long, unbroken roof that distinguishes this Cathedral. The aisle walls of the choir are also Norman for their first few feet, and twelfth-century masonry survives above the pointed arches of the choir.

The oldest work is below the Lady Chapel, for the foundations are partly those of the Saxon cathedral. It was a separate church, lying eastward of the Norman cathedral; there was space between the two to accommodate the elongation (from east to west) that the church underwent for a hundred years from about 1270.

The transformation of Exeter's east end followed the sequence carried out at Worcester in the earlier part of the thirteenth century. A start was made in the extreme east (on virgin ground at Worcester); there followed the building over of a space that had lain outside the eastern termination of a Romanesque choir. Finally came the grafting of the new work on to the older fabric and the altering of that older building into a semblance of the new. Exeter, with work started under Bishop Bronescombe, came late in a series of similar transformations and lengthenings out.

It was an almost continuous process. It does not seem that Bronescombe had seen much finished when he died in 1280. The bishops who commissioned the main work east of the towers were Quivil (1280–91), Bitton (1292–1307), and Stapledon (1308–26).

The earliest work, belonging to the comparatively simple "geometrical" phase of architecture, is the Lady Chapel with its two flanking chapels at its western end; the choir aisles with their projecting chapels (each with two altars) were also begun in Bronescombe's time. The Lady Chapel has its English, squared east end and a low roof recalling Hereford or Salisbury rather than Worcester. The tracery has the stiff, not wholly attractive character of its geometrical style; below the windows some tomb recesses contain effigies of early bishops. West of the chapel, and still with a lower vault, is an aisle-like vestibule; to this belongs the single pillar one sees behind the High Altar, clustered with sixteen shafts of Purbeck marble and simply moulded caps, the pattern and precursor of all the "Exeter pillars" of the Cathedral arcades. The lines were early determined along which all the remaining work of rebuilding was to be done. At the same time work went forward on the aisle walls and flanking chapels of the new structure (*novum opus*) that was to close the gap.

The outer walls, and the main structure of the presbytery that came next in the sequence, could still be built without pulling down the Norman apse; the old choir was untouched, for mediaeval builders nearly always planned so as to make it possible for services to continue, with no more annoyance than noise and dust, in the existing churches. This happened at Exeter while the canons were being given a far longer, more spacious eastern limb for their choir offices (in the choir) and for the celebration of High Mass (in the presbytery, or the part of the church reserved for the liturgical activity pertaining only to *presbyteri*, or priests). The next section, namely the four bays of the presbytery, was in its first form the most archi-tecturally advanced work ever put into the Cathedral. The bishop for most of the time was Bitton, his master mason one Roger; the work seems to have been done by 1304.

The aisle vaults were finished to a simple, "quadripartite" plan that has its contrast in the magnificently branching, embossed vault of the presbytery and choir. Then in those four eastern bays the builders kept to the design now becoming fashionable, and expres-sive of the vertical tendency that had become a feature of mediaeval architecture. Their aim was to overcome the feeling of inadequate height, so marked in the average English cathedral or abbey with its three storeys of main arcade, triforium gallery, and clerestory windows above (Exeter has an interior seriously deficient in height, and needed all they could do for it). So here, like earlier designers at Southwell and Pershore, they cut out the middle, or triforium, stage; they thus produced an effect of soaring, advanced design, undone later and to some extent spoilt when the choir triforium was extended over the entire eastern limb. Aiding the architects were the carvers, setting the fashion, here as all through the Cathedral, for extreme beauty and delicacy of detail, especially in bosses and wedge-shaped corbels with their lovely figures and foliage, to offset the modest scale of the building itself. Their work is the greatest glory of Exeter; along with the varied, still geometrical tracery of the upper windows and the marvellously rich furnishings of choir and presbytery they made of this eastern limb an object lesson in the mediaeval English tendency to excel in detail and miniature rather than in grandeur or sheer scale.

Next came the virtual rebuilding of the Norman choir. The arches were replaced below the original walls by those of the usual Exeter pattern, the walls, as one sees in the triforium, being thicker, and the pillars of greater diameter than in the presbytery. But a change, more conventional than in Roger's presbytery design, was made when a shallow, somewhat purposeless triforium of shafts and little arches was put above the richly moulded main arcade. As earlier at Worcester, the recasting of the choir was less successful than the wholly new work to the east. To ensure the uniformity so dear to Exeter designers, the triforium was then carried through the rest of the eastern limb. At the choir's west end a tiny extra bay with a pair of miniature, acutely pointed arches allows for the width of a choir screen that does not greatly impinge on the main arcades. By this time, too, the towers had become real transepts by being thrown into the body of the church, a crossing bay was created, and in default of a true triforium the narrow passages were run round the tower walls as galleries held up by delicately ribbed and corbelled vaults.

The eastern limb was completed by Bishop Stapledon. Here in particular one saw, and can still see, that delicate magnificence of detail that was favoured in English churches and which at Exeter received specially glorious expression. For between the choir screen and reredos the church was packed with a dazzling array of architectural adornment in wood or stone. To the coloured sculpture of bosses and corbels, and the brilliance of the windows, there was added a choice complement of tombs and liturgical equipment that made the canons occupants, if not of a vast architectural space, then at least of a choir whose beauty had few equals, so Grandisson said, in England or France (14).

The mediaeval choir had its western screen, its stalls, and throne, the presbytery some bishops' tombs and the sanctuary fittings, in particular the sedilia and the gorgeous altar screen. There are still the actual seats of the stalls, the throne, the western screen, the tombs in a somewhat mutilated state, the sedilia, and a few pin/ nacled fragments of the altar screen.

The seats with their misericords, incorporated into Victorian stallwork, are the oldest furnishings of all; indeed they are the oldest misericords in England. They date from the middle of the thirteenth century, their carvings being vigorous and simple, with little embellishment in addition to the main subjects. The subjects them/ selves are in many cases drawn from "bestiaries", but there are also foliage, knights, and other human figures. Perhaps the most famous English misericord is the "Exeter elephant", the animal having head, trunk, and tusks of the accepted African zoological pattern, but ending downwards in gigantic hoofed feet(3).

The screen, or *pulpitum*, is exceedingly lovely, with three shallow ogee arches, a vaulted passageway, a wealth of delicate fourteenth/ century foliage carving, and then an upper row of small arches whose spaces now have seventeenth/century Bible paintings but at first had sculptured panels. The screen had central doors and was meant to be a solid barrier between nave and choir; unhappily the spaces on each side have had their stone backing taken away and filled transparently with glass.

East of the stalls is the throne, its enclosure meant for a bishop's chair and flanking seats, the upper structure, a complex, gorgeous, symmetrical creation of canopies, image brackets, and tabernacle work that rises fifty/seven feet to a tapering, crocketed, spire/like terminal. Exeter certainly has the finest bishop's throne in Britain; the work was that of Robert of Galmpton (in Devon) and was being done in 1316.

Finally, the sanctuary has its sedilia, the amazingly delicate stone canopies perhaps later than the actual seats, the image brackets now capped by modern figures of Leofric, Edward the Confessor, and Queen Editha. The sedilia are not recessed in a wall, nor have they a solid backing to their seats, they stand free as do the canopies over such tombs as Edward II's at Gloucester. The sedilia, too, are of the early fourteenth century; they were only a pale shadow of the canopied and pinnacled glory that stood behind the High Altar.

For across the presbytery, high enough to obscure the two cross arches and their pillar, the craftsmen of the 1320's placed a superb altar screen. Its design, a combination of pinnacles, niches, and other architectural work in miniature, was similar to that of the smaller sedilia. But it must also have allowed for an altarpiece, and we hear of a silver panel, perhaps with the Coronation of the Virgin as its subject. The nearest parallel to this brilliant work must have been the surviving altar screen erected fifty years later at Durham.

On our way to the nave we see in the north tower the famous "Orrery" or mediaeval clock, without the diversion of knights or quarter jacks but with two dials that record not only the time of day but the supposed revolutions of the moon and sun round the Earth. We find a similar clock at Ottery, but which came first I cannot say.

Another, and greater link between Ottery and Exeter comes with the bishop who rebuilt the bulk of Exeter's nave. For Grandisson was responsible for this work and also for the transformation of Ottery Church. At Exeter, however, he was closer bound by patterns left by earlier bishops and their masons, and his cathedral architecture (supervised by Thomas of Witney) was less original than what he commissioned in his collegiate foundation; had Bishop Berkeley, with his strong family links with St. Augustine's Abbey, Bristol, lived longer the story might have been otherwise.

The rebuilding of the nave between the Norman aisle walls therefore closely followed the design that Stapledon's masons had started in the choir; only in the aisles are the more complex ribbed vaults a contrast to their simpler counterparts in the choir aisles. The same triforium is there as well as the "Exeter pillars", the same rich vaulting and similar corbels and bosses. Only the more westerly windows are different in that they have more "flowing" tracery than that in the eastern limb; it seems that these were erected in the 1350's after an interruption due to the Black Death. The main fabric may have been finished by 1360; it was late enough to have used the early Perpendicular of Gloucester, but precedent had kept the nave conservatively to the design laid down nearly a century before. One delightful feature, however, is all its own. For in one bay, at the triforium level on the north side, is the gallery for the minstrels with its projecting front. A row of canopied niches has a

21   The Nave, Screen and Organ

22   From the Air (taken before the War)

EXETER CATHEDRAL

23 Exeter: At Cowley Bridge, 1813
James Green, Architect

small orchestra of standing angels, each with a different instrument and combining to produce visual as well as imagined musical harmony(21).

The nave leads naturally to the west front(1), and here is the Cathedral's one unhappy artistic blunder. For the angles of clerestory and aisles are partly filled, in an attempt to create a great screen for sculpture in the manner of Salisbury, with panelled walls that merely slope downwards and emphasise the falsity of the device. The west window has good Decorated tracery, but below is another work that only partially succeeded, for all the goodness of its detail. The statue screen across the west end is of the late fourteenth century, partly from Grandisson's time, partly later. It would be more appropriate, and certainly better preserved, were it an interior choir screen like the great one at York. Its two main tiers of figures in their canopied niches at one time had as their chief statues the Coronation of the Virgin, with a company of apostles, prophets, and kingly personages to do honour to the central group.

The west front takes us to the beginnings of true Perpendicular; at the eastern end the new east window, of nine lights and put up in 1388-92, is wholly of the newer style. The top storey of the north tower is also Perpendicular, but from late in the fifteenth century with its window arches assimilated to the Norman work below. The remaining Perpendicular work is in such minor construction as chapel screens and chantries. Near the eastern end of the presbytery aisles is the pair of chantries put up by Bishop Oldham and by the Spekes of Whitelackington. Their elaborate screens are a version, but of early sixteenth-century date, of others in the Cathedral; the chapels are small projections from the aisles, but the screens and their rich decoration of panelling and vault make them appear more as interior furniture than architectural addition. Oldham's chantry has his vested effigy, a reredos whose central panel shows the Mass of St. Gregory, and badges of the owl that was a pun on the bishop's name and on his Lancashire home town.

Exeter Cathedral saw much furnishing and embellishment between the sixteenth century and the onset of Victorian restorations. It was remarkable for its constant, close, conservative adherence to the Gothic tradition; only in the splendid organ case of the early part of Charles II's reign, and then in the font, was there a departure from the earlier style.

Altars, statues, and much glass fell early victims, but many of the mediaeval fittings survived till the Puritan triumph. An exception was the altar screen. To replace it, Archdeacon Hellyar in 1638–9 commissioned William Cavell to paint a curious altarpiece in the Gothic vein; it was done in perspective to show the central space and two aisles of a Gothic cathedral.

The Puritans were drastic in their handling of the Cathedral. The mediaeval stalls were cast out and other artistic damage was done. The church was divided between Presbyterians and Independents. A solid wall to part them was run up from the choir screen to the roof; the resulting places of austere worship were known as "East Peter's" and "West Peter's", a new door being made in the Speke chantry to give access to the former.

The wall was destroyed at the Restoration, but blocks of box pews remained facing each other in the nave. A delightful, surviving, completely Baroque addition came in 1684 when the marble font and its cover were made; it is one of the choice gems of Exeter and recalls those installed in the London churches of Wren. The choir got new fittings that lasted till the nineteenth century. A canopied pulpit has now disappeared,* but the panelling behind the stalls, of considerable charm in a romantic Gothic vein, is now in large measure preserved round the hall of the Deanery. Then in 1818 the local architect and "statuary" Kendall (his firm made many murals for Exeter churches) put a delicately Gothic, by no means ineffective, altar screen across the whole east end; this was swept away in the 1870's in favour of Scott's reredos which is now at Heavitree. The stalls, too, were replaced by Scott with a canopied set whose design reflected the early fourteenth century.

By 1900 the Cathedral was essentially as it remained till 1942. Then in the air raid of May 4th the Cathedral became the only one of our pre-Reformation foundation to have a hit, direct on its main fabric, by a high explosive bomb. Mercifully the bomb did not strike the main choir vault, but fell, less harmfully for the main

---

* Its successor, installed in 1952, was given by The Exeter Free Churches; its style is imitatively that of fifteenth-century Devon wood pulpits.

structure, on the projecting St. James' chapel with its Treasury above. Chapel and Treasury were demolished, and with them three bays of the vault in the south choir aisle. The screenwork in the presbytery was smashed, the bulk of the Cathedral's glass was blown out. Since the war the aisle has been wholly restored, a mediaeval boss being found intact among the rubble and so replaced. The late Mr. Herbert Read worked lovingly to piece together the wooden screens; the chapel and Treasury are being rebuilt as before (the chapel being finished by now), and a new west window has replaced the Edwardian memorial glass to Frederick Temple.

The old glass had luckily been stored away, so Exeter remains moderately rich in this adornment. Some battered figures and canopies are in one early Decorated clerestory window of the choir, and "geometrical" windows of the eastern chapels have heraldic glass that comes, with its record of Grandisson alliances, from that bishop's time. The main collection, making up a curious variety, is in the early Perpendicular east window. For the figures, their canopies in a golden colour, and their heraldry from the early fourteenthcentury east window, are preserved from the older glazing of Stapledon's time. But to fill the three extra lights the glazier Robert Lyen made canopied figures of distinctly "Perpendicular" character, their canopies being silver and the saints being later in style. The window's heraldry, too, is a mixture, some being of the fourteenth and some, like the Neville shield, well into the following century.

Mediaeval glazing does not complete the story. In the eighteenth century William Peckitt of York was employed on restoration work, and in 1766 filled the west window with heraldic glass. Many of his panels are now in the modern "Cloister room", and the Deanery hall, with its panels of the Royal Arms in their various phases, has more Peckitt glass of 1762 and 1768; the whole collection is among our more interesting Georgian glazing.

Nor is Exeter devoid of that mediaeval wallpainting that must have been a splendid, colourful adornment in the Cathedral as in smaller churches. There is the Resurrection from above the Sylke chantry, but far lovelier is the Coronation of the Virgin whose painting is set in the head of an arched recess in the vestibule to the

Lady Chapel. Both of these paintings are probably of the late fifteenth century.

The earliest bishops' monuments are in many ways those of most artistic interest. One in the Lady Chapel, a somewhat crudely sculptured figure, in low relief and below a triangular-headed canopy, may be that of Leofric, though some years later than 1072. In any case it seems certain to be one of our earliest English bishop's effigies. Of greater distinction is the early thirteenth-century effigy, sculptured in Purbeck marble and in high relief on a raised and panelled tomb, of Bishop Marshall (d. 1206). At the end of the century came the splendidly coloured, gracefully vested effigy of Bronescombe, recumbent and resting beneath its own little canopy in relief. Its elaborate architectural canopy, to the same design as that of Bishop Stafford which lies opposite, was not raised till the fifteenth century. Stapledon's figure in the sanctuary is below a shallow-arched canopy that clearly recalls the artist of the bishop's choir screen, and Bishop Berkeley's simple tomb once had a half-length brass. Grandisson's tomb no longer survives, but he lay in the tiny chapel wedged between the nave and the inside of the western image-screen. Bishop Stafford (d. 1419) has an effigy of great splendour and distinction(6), but other pre-Reformation bishops like Bothe and Veysey are buried away from Exeter. One need not say much of the memorials to post-Reformation holders of the See; to my mind the best is the Georgian-Renaissance composition in memory of Bishop Weston (1724–42); it seems to have been by his namesake whose work we shall notice in Exeter churches.

The most interesting priests' memorials are the early Tudor "cadavers" to Precentor Sylke (d. 1508) and Canon Parkhouse (d. 1540); the latter's recessed canopy brings us to the verge of Renaissance art, and a neighbouring civilian tomb to Anthony Harvey (d. 1564) has fully Renaissance decoration, though in the main a late survival of the mediaeval tradition. The better of the Cathedral's two brasses is also to a priest, for it shows the coped, kneeling figure of Canon Langton (d. 1413), a relative of Bishop Stafford, and in the heraldry of his brass acknowledging his preferment. There are also some tombs of armed mediaeval knights, chiefly in the south transept to Hugh Courtenay, 2nd Earl of

Devon (d. 1377) and his lady; the tomb was once in a separate chantry in the nave. An Elizabethan-Renaissance group, gay with proudly multiplied heraldry, keeps bright the memory of the Carews, and another monument is to Sir John Gilbert, half-brother to Raleigh. But the most beautiful Renaissance monument is in the south aisle of the choir. For there an exquisitely sensitive portrait bust starts out from an oval, wreathed frame to commemorate another bishop's relative, Canon Edward Cotton who was Cathedral treasurer and died in 1675; his father had been precentor and his grandfather the bishop from 1598 to 1621 (17). The best of the "Regency" memorials is Flaxman's to General Simcoe (d. 1806), with its statues set in a Gothic setting unusual for this sculptor.

A secular cathedral did not greatly need cloisters, but it became the fashion to have them, and Exeter's, pulled down by the Puritans and partly rebuilt in our own time, were early Perpendicular of the late fourteenth century. But a Chapter House was essential, and here it was south of the Cathedral. It is rectangular, as in many abbeys, of two distinct periods, and therefore of architectural note. For the lower part, including the west door and a sumptuously shafted range of wall arcading (with much fourteenth-century painting), is Early English from soon after 1225. But in another two centuries the Chapter House was in bad condition and must have seemed too low inside. For its upper stage was pulled down and another, loftier top storey was built about 1413–20. The newer work rises past shafts and canopied niches to a splendid timber roof; at the east end the sun pours in through a great transomed window of seven lights.

The Palace and Deanery stand south-east and south-west of the Cathedral. The former is rambling, partly of the thirteenth century, with late Perpendicular additions and some Georgian alterations inside, but essentially and with little change a mediaeval pile. A noteworthy, bomb-blasted feature is the Early English chapel which Bishop Temple completely transformed. For in 1878–9 he commissioned Butterfield in his most typical and drastic mood to recast and refurnish it with a new screen, a white marble cross behind the altar, and a varied riot of multi-coloured tiles. The result, undreamed of by the mediaeval bishops, was a quintessential expression of Victorian taste.

The Deanery is in all ways more satisfying. We have glanced already at its panelling and glass; the actual building has the two original, parallel blocks of the thirteenth century, remodelled a century later with tracery and waggon roofs in the chapel and room adjoining. The hall of the fifteenth century has its graceful, arch/braced roof with delicate finials to adorn a fine ceremonial apart/ment. Below it a room with Jacobean panels and plaster frieze has an ornate fireplace put in by Veysey when he was Dean (1509–19).

The Close was separately fortified with towered gates and build/ings clinging, as still they do, to the perimeter of its outer walls. The houses of some clerical dignitaries lay along the northern side; the treasurer's touched the north tower of the Cathedral itself. The sequence of buildings, a trifle untidy and including the Courtenays' town house (now, with a lovely, skylit Regency library, the Devon and Exeter Institution), has some houses rebuilt in the eighteenth century and one a splendid early Georgian work with its heraldic rainwater heads. A house that was the Archdeacon of Barnstaple's has a charming inner courtyard behind a Jacobean oak door. At another point a fifteenth/century doorway with the Chancellor's Arms leads to a house whose mediaeval hall has a traceried, angel/dight, hammerbeam roof. Behind the early Georgian house a hall of about 1500 with a stone fireplace and simple waggon roof was that of the "Annuellars" or priests who said the chantry Requiems in the Cathedral. On the other side of the Close, between St. Mary Major's and the Deanery, there once stood the most picturesque feature of all, the enclosure first called "Calendarhay" after the brotherhood of the Calendars, but then the Exeter equivalent to the famous Vicars' Close at Wells.

The tenure of a secular canonry meant no obligation to reside so long as a canon appointed a *vicarius* to fill his place (*vicem*) during his permanent or temporary non/residence. These "vicars choral" thus did much of the routine work whereby the daily choir services were maintained. They were often young, not in priest's orders, in great need of discipline and ordered life. In most secular cathedrals they were sooner or later gathered together so as to live in "colleges" (the very word means "gathering together" without educational significance); at Hereford and Wells their buildings are nearly intact. At Exeter the reform came under Bishop Brantingham. Two parallel rows of cottages were built down the two sides of a long narrow court, much as one sees them now at Wells but on a smaller scale. At one end was a gate, at the other a hall. So the college long survived, altered, insanitary, picturesque, till the last houses were pulled down in the nineteenth century. Only the hall remained, with its Renaissance panelling and mediaeval stonework. It was gutted by the bombs in 1942, but in its ruins the tracery, transomed windows, and cusped rere-arches still proclaim a date about 1390.

Chapter IV

EXETER
CHURCHES, CHARITIES, HOUSES, COMMERCE

NOT one of Exeter's religious houses vied with the size or splendour of the Cathedral. Most of them have disappeared; of two alone are there important remains.

Over the Exe the small Benedictine priory of Cowick was first a dependency of Bec Abbey in Normandy; then in the fifteenth century, when the last of these "alien priories" were seized as "enemy property" and their lands made over to English religious foundations, it was disputed between Eton College and Tavistock Abbey, in the end becoming a "cell" of Tavistock. St. James' Priory, downstream from the city and on the same side of the river, was from about 1164 a small dependency of the Cluniac St. Martin's, Paris. It was eventually made over, along with its tithes in the "Prior's" portion of Tiverton parish, to King's College, Cambridge. There were also the two friaries, Franciscan and Dominican. The former eventually settled on a site outside South Gate; their names survive in Friary Walk. The Dominicans, as we have seen, were on the site later that of Bedford House and Bedford Circus.

St. Nicholas' Priory, with early Norman origins, had buildings that were an excellent example of a small Benedictine convent. The church was cruciform, the cloister had a projecting, octagonal *lavatorium*, or washing place, of a type rare in England but found in Lewes Priory, and abroad at Sicilian Monreale. The important remains are in the western range, a building later used for various secular purposes, including minting and the touching of silver with the three-towered castle (from the City Arms) of the Exeter Assay mark. The range included cellarage (partly in the vaulted Norman rooms that can still be seen), an impressive kitchen with simply

24 Baptist Chapel, Little Britain, 1817

25 George's Meeting, South Street, 1761

EXETER NONCONFORMITY

26 Free Cottages, 1861⁄3. St. Michael's, by Rhode Hawkins, 1867⁄8

27 Upper Market, by Fowler, 1838

AT EXETER

arched fireplaces, a guest hall whose timber roof and Perpendicular windows speak of fifteenth-century reconstruction, and the quarters of the Prior which partly occupy some finely finished Perpendicular additions made to an essentially Norman building. There are also the changes made when the block, of domestic character and meant for living, was readily converted into a Tudor house.

The position is similar at the small Benedictine nunnery of Polslo. This was a late Norman foundation, never large, but mediaeval Exeter's one place where women could fulfil a religious vocation. The church was perhaps a simple rectangular building as at Lacock Abbey (nuns needed no side-chapels for private masses); it has perished, along with the cloisters and two sides of the buildings, but here again the western range, being domestic in character, survived to become a house. The main features are the gabled buttresses of early thirteenth-century type, the upstairs guest hall of the same period with its original wooden buttery screen, and the Prioress' room with its hooded fireplace like those of the thirteenth century at Lacock.

We are little better off for remains of Exeter's old hospitals and almshouses. Of the former the most important was the twelfth-century hospital of St. John; the buildings near Eastgate were spared at the Dissolution, and then in the seventeenth century became a refounded almshouse and the early Grammar School, with cloth markets held in the buildings during Exeter's Fairs. They were a "picturesque" group, for the most part rebuilt at various times in Georgian Gothic. Now they have disappeared, and the Grammar School, like others such as Hele's, is in modern buildings elsewhere.

There are other almshouses, as one would expect in such a city, but only one still lays much claim to beauty or architectural charm. St. Catherine's was an attractive, rambling set of fifteenth-century buildings; the raids, however, reduced them to a shell. But Wynard's, another fifteenth-century charity, is in use (after modernisation) and has more to show. The founder, in 1430, was William Wynard; only a fine cross-arch in the chapel is recognisably of his time. For the almshouse had a chequered history, became decayed, and had to be rebuilt, in poorly wearing red sandstone, in the seventeenth century. But the mediaeval manner persisted, and the courtyard, off Magdalen Street, with cobbles and oak doorframes, makes it the most "picturesque" charity in Exeter. Nor should one forget some old foundations more conveniently rebuilt to suit modern needs. Notable among these are Attwill's, an Elizabethan foundation and originally sited near the present Central Station. They are now in New North Road, their twelve cottages rebuilt in excellent early Victorian Gothic and dated 1839. Along Magdalen Street the Magdalen Almshouses are now a Victorian Gothic range dated 1863, and near the road⁄fork known as Liverydole the Alms⁄ houses founded in the 1590's by Sir Robert and Sir Thomas Dennis retain their Tudor chapel but had their dwellings rebuilt in sightly late Perpendicular which is dated 1849.

More interesting, indeed a remarkable piece of last century's zeal to provide in an orderly manner for "industrious poor", are the Free Cottages of 1861–3; their architecture is a piece with the larger, contemporary, adjoining block of Bishop Blackhall's (rebuilt) Charity School. A magnificent site between the city's northern defensive valley and St. David's Church was given by one John Dinham. The cottages were laid out so as to command the views towards Haldon and over the Exe. They are in four neat, carefully planned rows with a broad central avenue liberally planted with the trees and shrubs of Victorian landscape taste, their style is red brick Tudor with mullions and little double porches; they and the schools, with their great Dutch gable, are dominated by the tower and spire of St. Michael's (26).

Exeter's mediaeval parish churches have been drastically reduced and rebuilt. Of those, including St. Thomas' (the apostle, but earlier of Canterbury) that existed before the Reformation, St. George's, St. Paul's, All Hallows Goldsmith Street, St. Kerrian's, and All Hallows⁄on⁄the⁄Wall were pulled down, St. Sidwell's (rebuilt in the Gothic of the Regency), St. Lawrence's (which was small and unaisled), and St. John's (already disused and decaying) were irretrievably bombed, St. David's has been twice rebuilt, St. Edmund's, St. Mary Major, and Holy Trinity once each; the last is interesting early nineteenth⁄century Gothic by Kendall, with a good west front and fine iron lampholders. There remain St. Mary

Arches, St. Pancras', St. Mary Steps, St. Petrock's, St. Stephen's, St. Martin's, St. Olave's, and St. Thomas'.

As architecture they are not impressive, having suffered more than most town churches from that fragmentation into poor, tiny parishes that was characteristic of mediaeval English cities. Mediaeval Exeter was less prosperous than the city later became, and no one parish was predominant like St. Peter Mancroft, at Norwich. They are therefore puny, their main material a pleasingly coloured yet crumbling red sandstone; they are distinguished by their miniature Perpendicular towers, whereof that of St. Olave's is so narrow that it fills no more than half the width of the aisle into which it descends (the same church's Perpendicular arcades are by no means without graceful beauty). But the best architecture is in St. Mary Arches and St. Petrock's. As other early mediaeval churches in Exeter were devoid of arcades or aisles, the former took its name from its arches, which are admirable late Norman, with their round pillars and "scalloped" capitals (35). At St. Petrock's we have a charming tower whose top stage is an octagon, and a new chancel built out towards the Close, "reorientating" the church so that one looks to the altar *across* the exquisite Perpendicular arcades with their capitals crowned with angels; we know that Bishop Chard consecrated the church in 1513. St. Martin's has a large Perpendicular west window, and at St. Stephen's the ground space is so restricted that the chancel crosses an alley by an arch or "bow".

However, the churches have some pre-Reformation contents to compensate for architectural modesty. The Norman fonts at St. Pancras (plain) and St. Mary Steps (more elaborately moulded) (13), the latter church's well-known mid-Tudor clock and jacks, the late fifteenth-century screen, with its crudely painted panels of saints, now in St. Mary Steps but said originally to have been in St. Mary Major, all these make up a collection well worth seeing. The one really good pre-Reformation tomb is of Thomas Andrews (d. 1518) in St. Mary Arches; like Greenway of Tiverton he was a Merchant Adventurer of London and the Company's Arms accompany his effigy, but the religious sculpture was deliberately scraped away. The same church has curious Georgian ironwork which combines a mayoral sword-rest and a crane for the font cover, also one of the Exeter churches' many achievements of the Royal Arms. This one is of Charles II, but the collection ranges from his father to the Hanoverians.

There are font covers and altar rails of varying Renaissance periods, while St. Martin's is rightly proud of its delightfully Baroque sanctuary fittings of Bishop Blackhall's (1708–16) time; among them are three-sided altar rails and benches for communicants gathered round them. Where, however, these Exeter churches surpass is in their mural monuments. The largest group is to Elizabethan and seventeenth-century merchants. St. Mary Arches and St. Petrock's are specially well filled; three in the latter church are clearly by the same hand. One in St. Martin's is of the interesting "Barnstaple" school,* and in St. Mary Major that to Sir Benjamin Olliver (d. 1672) is admirably, massively Baroque with its twisted columns. Many late Georgian murals are by the Kendall firm, and in St. Martin's a particularly fine, emotional Grecian composition by Baily is to a young lady who died in 1826. The most interesting group, Baroque in inspiration and uniform in style, is by Exeter's own sculptor, John Weston. His most striking work is in St. Petrock's, moved there from the demolished St. Kerrian's. For below a composition to Jonathan Ivie (d. 1717) is a plaque in relief of a subject amazing at such a date, for it vividly shows the General Resurrection and Last Judgment; it is hardly less remarkable when one knows that Weston did a similar plaque for a lawyer's monu-ment at Whitchurch near Tavistock(12).

St. Thomas' is more spacious than the city churches; it is, in fact, by reason of its site in what was really a village outside the walls, a country church. The main fabric was much reconstructed in the seventeenth century, as also was the fine Perpendicular tower. East of the nave are Gothic transepts and a chancel in a stately composi-tion unusually fine for their early nineteenth-century date; of greater architectural interest is the Carew Chapel of about 1680, a blend of Gothic, fan-vaulted and with pendents in wood, and of classical detail. The eagle lectern of the fifteenth century is Exeter's best piece of church woodwork outside the Cathedral. Here, too, are good mural monuments, one perhaps by Weston is to Thomas

* See Katharine A. Esdaile, *English Church Monuments, 1510–1840*, p. 123.

Northmore, M.P. (d. 1713), of the family that gave Pugin his two last Christian names; another commemorates General Gordon's grandfather.

The present St. David's, built about 1900 to a sturdy, impressive design by Caroë, had a predecessor of 1816, a severely Doric, porticoed design with a western cupola; it was by J. D. Green, and strictly in the London manner of Smirke and Inwood. St. Mary Major, a rebuild of 1865–7 by Edward Ashworth, has been much reviled and with some justice, but its arcade of stone and marble is a good Victorian interpretation of Early English. Ashworth was cathedral architect, and designed all but the mediaeval tower of the church at Topsham, but the masterpiece of Exeter's Victorian church architecture is not his. St. Michael's, by Rhode Hawkins, and dating from 1867, is a brilliant, impressive composition in the geometrical Gothic favoured in Bronescombe's time. It is cruciform, with curiously narrow nave aisles that have shrines at their ends and no connection with the transepts. But its real glory is the pinnacled spire of the central steeple, not unworthy, in its commanding dignity, to challenge the towers of the Cathedral in the Exeter skyline.

Last among Exeter's major works in Victorian Gothic comes St. Luke's College, a lengthy range in mullioned Decorated that lies along the Heavitree road; it was by Hayward the local architect and is just a century old, a companion venture in religious education to the somewhat similar colleges at Cheltenham and in the Bristol suburb of Fishponds.

Of the Nonconformist churches "George's Meeting" (Unitarian) of 1760–1 has a pleasant red-brick front, a Roman Doric portico, and its original furnishings(25), while the Mint Methodist Chapel of 1812 has good points in its considerably altered façade. Best of all is the delightful Baptist Chapel (now a furniture store) in Little Britain. It was started in 1817, an exquisite Regency work with pediments and pillars, and decoration of wreaths that forms a close link with some of Exeter's contemporary villas that seem to be the works of the same designer-builder(24).

Exeter's domestic architecture of the Middle Ages is neither plentiful nor very distinctive. The tradition seems to have been that of the half/timbered house with its overhanging storeys. The one really effective group of such work is in Stepcote Hill, the houses combining with the stepped sidewalks and central, cobbled gutter of the steeply tumbling road to produce a truly antique and "pic/ turesque" ensemble. A different tradition, with at least a proportion of stone walling, survives in the back portions of such houses in the Close as that now well known as Tinley's café. But the city's best mediaeval domestic work is in the remains of St. Nicholas' and Polslo priories.

Nor are there very many Tudor or Stuart houses; Mol's Coffee House in the Close* and the upper storeys, above the plate/glass of the shop fronts, of some houses in High Street and Fore Street are the best examples, and other houses of the same periods are near the site of South Gate. Then in the last years of the seventeenth century came houses in which Professor Richardson has pointed out a Dutch influence, though without the curved gables of Topsham. The best, however, of Exeter's houses are undeniably Georgian.

Early Georgian, or even mid/eighteenth/century domestic archi/ tecture is comparatively scarce, and a residence like Mount Radford had more to be considered as a country domain than as a town house. I have, however, shown that there are some early Georgian houses in the Close, and others up and down the city, like St. Olave's Rectory, go back before George III's reign. By the 1760's a local tradition had grown up of domestic building in a sightly dark/red brick.

The next phase was that of developments and "improvement" as the commercial classes moved out from the older parts of the city, and as a "residential" element was added to the clerical and pro/ fessional population. Two distinct phases came in a sequence that lasted from the 1770's to the Regency.

To quote Alexander Jenkins, the "spirit of improvement began now to manifest itself" about 1768 when William Mackworth Praed built houses near High Street and also in the Close, the large inn and Assembly Room that later became the Royal Clarence; a less happy breath from the improving spirit was that which swept away the Tudor arched conduit that stood at the "Carfax" in the

---

* Prof. Pevsner usefully points out that its "Dutch" gable is Victorian.

middle of the city; the gates, too, fell gradual victims to the vista urge.

But the most important new feature was Bedford Circus, now wholly obliterated by bombing and replanning. It came as the first of many features in Georgian Exeter, nearly all of them on the eastern, comparatively level side of the old city. They owed much, in general inspiration and in detail, to the great wave of speculative building and estate improvement that was then transforming great London areas like Bloomsbury.

In the case of Bedford Circus the coincidence of Bloomsbury and Exeter was deliberately exact. For Bloomsbury and "Bedford Precinct" alike belonged to the Duke of Bedford, and it was in the 1770's that decisions were made to develop both the Bloomsbury estate and the area of Exeter then covered by the decaying, scarce-used mansion of Bedford House. The crucial year was 1773-4. A plan had been made some years before for a London Bedford Circus whose prototype was to be the circus at Bath. But when in 1774 the idea began to be fulfilled it was carried out as a square—the grass in the centre remaining, however, a round plot. In Exeter the plans allowed from the start of a graceful curvature. Bedford House was doomed to be pulled down (the foundations of the Dominican Friary being eventually found below), and in 1773 a building lease of the site was granted to Robert Stribling, a local builder and presumably the main designer of the northern side of the circus. For about thirty years his completed segment formed a crescent on its own, for the other side, its middle occupied by Bedford Chapel with its classical portico and its doorways graced with Ionic columns, was not built till the period of "Regency".

The northern side itself was slow in completing, for checks were imposed by the financial aspects of the American Revolutionary War. It was not finished till about 1790; as it stood till 1942 it remained a provincial builder's masterpiece in the later "Adam" taste.

Stribling's part of Bedford Circus had fourteen houses. Their frontage was in the dark-red brick now to be so prominent and characteristic of terrace houses in Exeter. The storeys were parted one from another by platbands of cream-painted stone, the windows were square-headed, the doors arched. But over each door, and supported by flanking pillars, were delicate little architraves with fluting in the manner of the 1780's. Some features later common in Exeter terraces were absent from this first portion of Bedford Circus. But if one takes the whole volume of Exeter's late Georgian achieve-ment it is notable how much is shared with work of the same period in London, and chiefly with Bloomsbury where there arose the speculative development of the Bedford estate. The house fronts, particularly in a range such as Barnfield Crescent, are very like those in London that were built after patterns in the builders' pattern books and conformed to the Building Act of 1774(28). The builders of London's Bedford Square had been users, for exterior adornment, of Coade's artificial stone. The same material is found copiously in Exeter, especially in the vividly grinning masks that grace the head of many a round-arched doorway. They could easily have come from London by sea, and many are clearly cast from the same moulds that were used for decorative work in the capital. There is also the habit, a pleasing diversion where ornament in the round was so sparingly used, of putting a course of darker coloured brick round the arches of doorways and ground-floor windows; the windows and doors themselves are often recessed by the width of one brick to give an extra effect of light and shade. In Bloomsbury the colour contrast is of red against the yellow (or grimy black) of London stock brick. In Exeter the same effect is obtained by two different shades of red. The general kinship seems beyond question, and Exeter Georgian, unlike the admirable eighteenth-century brick-work of Worcester or Bristol, became a locally adapted extension of that seen in residential London.

The actual process of development lasted till about 1815, and though there were never, as in Dublin, complete areas with succes-sive streets and squares, the total achievement was such as to create a "genteel" area within easy reach of Southernhay and to adorn Exeter with a distinguished collection of terrace architecture, often in small units, which added much to the city's accommodation and power to attract new residents.

Southernhay is a strip of grassland (used regularly for pasture as late as 1782) that lies immediately outside the line of the walls;

28   Exeter: In Barnfield Crescent, 1798-1800

AN ANALYSIS OF GEORGIAN

29   Pennsylvania Crescent, *c.* 1823

30   Custom House, 1678-81

31   In Southernhay, 1798-1802

EXETER MISCELLANY

the city itself was ground landlord as far out as the width of the town ditch. Along, and projecting eastwards from, this charm, ing area there grew up the Southernhay terraces, Dix's Field, and Barnfield Crescent. The district was also the site, in 1786, of Exeter's first theatre. Barnfield Crescent, a delightful range which seems to have been planned by a local builder called Nosworthy, comes midway, in point of style, between Bedford Circus which, like it, lacked the Coade stone masks, and such blocks as Colleton Crescent and some of the Southernhay terraces which have them in abundance, as also the window arches in two shades of red which lend great charm to Barnfield Cresent. The important period is 1790–1810; within those two decades the city gained the parallel blocks (now thinned by bombing) of Dix's Field, the Southernhay terraces (31), and groups like Lower Summerlands, and a few houses in Longbrook Street, at Heavitree, and along the Topsham road. Colleton Crescent is on a splendid site overlooking the river and canal; finally we have the highly distinguished Baring Place, with little Doric pillars to flank its doors and a general feeling akin to the (Ionic) work of the later segment once in Bedford Circus.

The operations in Southernhay will serve as an illustration of what occurred; Colleton Crescent of about 1798–1800 is almost contemporary and has similar details.

In 1792 proposals were made to the Council's Southernhay Committee for a row of houses according to a single plan and elevation; the actual builders were a more numerous body, and later in the 1790's we hear of John King, Joseph Rowe, and David Evans Phillips (the last, along with Messrs. Trewman and Richard Hughes, the builder of the theatre). It seems that the outbreak of war imposed delays, but leases were granted, house by house, between 1797 and 1802 for the upper terrace on the western side. The terrace opposite, with its Doric colonnade, is of about 1810; it was not long now before red, brick ranges gave way to Exeter's villa phase.

The city's Regency and Greek Revival architecture, like the terraces, is well scattered. In its own time it included some public buildings, but many of these have disappeared, and we are left, for the most part, with domestic work. The most interesting group of houses is, however, closely akin to the Baptist Chapel in Little Britain which is Exeter's best piece of Nonconformist architecture.

There are several delightful villas, notably at the far end of Magdalen Street and in the pairs of semi-detached houses that make up Pennsylvania Crescent (29), which have garlands and end pilasters with incised lines that point to their being the work of the Baptists' builder-designer of 1817; Professor Richardson gives 1823 as a date for Pennsylvania Crescent. Other similar villas are in Friary Walk, and the same, originally Franciscan, area of Friars' Hay has, in Colleton Villa with its Ionic porch, a notably good stuccoed house of the Greek Revival. All these are chaste, refined works; they would not be out of place in Cheltenham or Leamington. They come as delightful additions to the social and architectural wealth of mainly mediaeval Exeter.

The same period also contributed its more public buildings. A distinguished work, with subtle refinements among its panelling, shelves, and galleries, was the Library contrived to fill the yard space of the Courtenays' house when it became the home of the Devon and Exeter Institution. This was in 1813; the Library so produced, with its admirable cupola lighting from above, was like that designed by Foulston at Plymouth for the Proprietary Library, becoming in due course one of the saddest of Plymouth's air-raid losses.

Other Exeter buildings of this period have not survived. The Subscription Rooms of 1820 were near the New London Inn at the London end of High Street; they were by Burgess the local architect, and had a dignified façade whose centre was graced by two Ionic columns. Next year saw the completion, in Southernhay, of the Baths with their unusual, somewhat ornately composed, Grecian frontage by Lethbridge (7). In the meantime civil engineering work was in progress under J. D. Green whom we have noticed as the rebuilder of St. David's Church. The canal we shall study later, but out on the city's northern outskirts he did brilliantly in his three-arched design for the new Cowley Bridge (of 1813) that carries the Crediton road (23).

The first half of last century saw an important addition to Exeter's town plan. Northgate Street and Goldsmith Street being narrow and unsatisfactory, there arose a need for better access to the newly developed areas of residence. The railways, with St. David's (one of Brunel's Italianate designs for the South Devon Railway) and Queen Street (now Central) Stations, were soon to give another reason for a good road in this northerly direction. So late in the 1830's a completely new, and by Exeter standards a wide and impressive street was driven through the tangled territory across the High Street, as one went north-west from the Close. It was by now appropriate to call it Queen Street, and one would expect in it a mainly Victorian Gothic aspect, but the idiom of its earlier shopping blocks is still unquestionably that of the Grecian phase. An admirable, simple building is the Dispensary of 1840 by Samuel Greig; it replaced an original foundation of 1818. But the main adornment of Queen Street, indeed one of Exeter's finest buildings, is the pure Doric frontage of the Upper Market; it bears the date 1838(27).

Its designer was the most notable architect who ever came from Exeter. Charles Fowler was born there in 1792. He became the assistant, in London, of David Laing, who was Chief Surveyor to the Customs and designed the Custom Houses in London and Plymouth. Fowler himself became a specialist in the design of covered markets, with Doric columns and other classic features as their conscious adornments. He designed Covent Garden for the Duke of Bedford, and also Hungerford Market on the site of Charing Cross Station. But his native city was to see his best work, first the bombed Lower Market of 1835, then the masterpiece that survives.

The Queen Street end, being the chief, more monumental entrance, has fluted columns and an excellent pediment; at the back the columns are simpler and unfluted. Between the façades comes the market interior, its main feature a magnificent clerestoried hall with granite pillars of a plainer, less Grecian, more obviously utilitarian design. The whole is truly great architecture; were it larger one might almost compare the main entrance to Hardwick's great Euston approach.

Another building whose character is mainly commercial takes us well back from the thirties and forties of last century.

To outward appearance, the Tuckers' Hall in Fore Street is a modern Gothic building of modest size, for it has been wholly refaced. But its basic structure and waggon roof are those of a fifteenth-century Guild chapel and hall that became the premises of the Incorporated Weavers, Fullers, and Shearmen. Its present state it owes to alterations made under Charles I, when the building was subdivided into two storeys. The lower, of simple appearance, was the school for teaching the sons of members. The upper is the hall for business and convivial occasions. The rich panelling in the Carolean taste, profuse, barbaric, uninfluenced by the pure classicism of Inigo Jones, bears the date 1637, the overmantel is one year later. The whole interior is one of Exeter's best, remarkably genuine in its feeling and expressive of the solid prosperity of the city's chief trade.

Downhill, and towards the river, lies the old industrial area, with two Georgian factory buildings near Trew's Weir; down river, too, is the port which made its own contribution to Exeter's engineering and architecture.

We have seen how Exeter's canal of the 1560's was the earliest of our artificial inland waterways. The first of its three building phases produced a modest engineering achievement not now visible, or indeed recognisable, in the canal of today. For the depth was only three feet; it allowed access to the city of no craft larger than small lighters, and there had to be transhipment at Topsham of goods in the trade overseas. The canal gave trouble from its earliest days, and by 1581, despite a new ashlar-fronted quay and the thoughtful provision of a crane, the City Fathers complained bitterly of the expense they had borne and of the understandably small use that had so far been made of their cherished watercourse.

The only solution lay in a drastic enlargement, not merely in a lengthening of the canal. In Charles II's reign it was indeed extended to a point across the river from Topsham, and sundry other improvements gave hopes that more shipping would reach the city itself. So in 1678 an agreement was made for the building of the present Custom House. It was finished by 1682, and a rainwater head is dated 1681. The accommodation was shared, by an agreement of 1683, between the Custom Officer and his officials and the civic authority of the port.

The Custom House, as it stands on the Old Quay, is surely one of England's most delightful buildings devoted to this particular purpose, an excellent minor work in the vernacular brickwork of the age of Wren, its outward aspect a blend of mellow red brick and the creamy paint of its stone dressings and window-frames. A pediment contains the Stuart Royal Arms; the ground-floor storey consisted at first of an open arcade, now filled by Georgian brick walls (30). Within, the balustraded staircase has above it a plasterwork ceiling with a circular panel and foliage in the four corners, and the Long Room ceiling, with its rich foliate oval, its pattern of the oak leaf, and an assortment of descending branches, is an effective, if somewhat crudely opulent essay in a Baroque vein more perfectly achieved in many contemporary mansions.

But the real improvement of the canal was set afoot at the very end of the century. The time was one when great prospects opened before the cloth traders of East Devon. For Dutch William's policy, naturally enough, was one of increased trade with the Netherlands and so to the Dutch ports' hinterlands in central Europe. In 1696 the Exeter Council appointed a committee for making the canal navigable for ships of up to a hundred tons. The actual scheme, of 1698, was for a drastic improvement; it also envisaged that the channel should be taken down to its present lower entrance at Turf. One William Bailey of Winchester was engaged as engineer; his scheme was bold, allowing for a ship canal whose depth and capacity would have had no rival among the inland waterways of his time. It was also to include, as its one lock, a small basin entered at each end by "double locks" (in other words with two gates, not merely a single sluice). The intervening space was to be large enough to hold several ships at a single passage. The depth of the canal was to be as much as fourteen feet; the other dimensions, and the scale of the necessary works, were to be generous in proportion.

But Bailey's ideas had over a century to wait for their fulfilment. It may be that not enough money was ever allowed him for the completion of so great a work of civil engineering; in any case he "fled" in 1699 and one Daniel Dennett succeeded him. The work was slowly completed and on a smaller scale, only ten feet deep instead of the fourteen allowed for in Bailey's scheme. At last it was opened in 1725, the distinguished visitors on a gaily auspicious occasion including Archbishop Blackburne of York (he had been Exeter's own bishop from 1717 to 1724) and the Exeter-born Lord Chief Justice (later Lord Chancellor) King. The only visible relic that I have spotted of this early eighteenth-century canal is the charm-ing little brick building that is now the Double Locks Inn, but which may first have been built as a house for the sluice-keeper (an agreement for such a house was made in 1701). With its steeply sloping roof it strongly recalls, in a simple, more rustic idiom, the delightful *waaghuizen* of some Dutch towns which themselves had so powerfully influenced the Custom House at King's Lynn. As it stands by the lock gates with its attendant trees it makes a charming picture of almost East Anglian riparian peace; behind in the distance are Warelwast's twin towers to beckon us citywards and to a succession of the finest views of the Cathedral.

But the canal as now used, extending down to Turf and of about the width and depth suggested by Bailey in 1698, is the work, from 1819 to about 1830, of James Green. The old canal had given frequent trouble and had been affected by the tidal flow; in any case it would not take all Exeter's shipping, and Topsham had remained the chief port on the Exe. So Green carried out the final series of improvements, and the canal architecture which we now see is mainly of his time. The lockhouse at Turf and the tollhouse, partly polygonal and of stone, at Countess Weir have "Regency" charac-ter and considerable vernacular charm, while at its Exeter end the canal finishes in a basin of ample size that recalls the contemporary Gloucester dock. Two of the warehouses are of the 1830's, and then, across the ferry that spans the delightful stretch of artificially im-proved river known in old times as "The Broad", comes the lower end of the quay and on it two more warehouses of the same period, magnificent examples of the commercial building of their time. One of them is dated 1835 and bears the name of Mayor De La Garde who was a keen sponsor and early historian of Exeter's port develop-ment (9). This warehouse is probably the one whose builder was Robert Stribling Cornish; if his second Christian name came from a marriage between a Cornish and a member of the family whence originated the first builder of Bedford Circus, then here we find in this warehouse designer a last flowering of the Georgian building tradition whose greatest work had been the most dignified single feature of the city's select quarter.

Churches and charities apart, the Victorians added not a little to the volume of Exeter's architecture. No longer in the front rank of industry and trade, the city remained of a modest size, with 23,479 people in 1821 and 37,568 in another seventy years. But it became a great transport centre once railways had reached it, and Plymouth and Devonport's expansion did not impair the dignity or pride of this cathedral city and county town on the other side of Devonshire.

We have seen how Queen Street was started as an important new thoroughfare; by the time its most prominent building arose it was in the age and style of Albertine commemoration. So the Victoria and Albert Memorial Museum of 1865-9, the earliest element in a foundation that also helped towards the beginnings of the University College, is a work by John Hayward in the most assertive of pink and grey Victorian Gothic. Along the road the Rougemont Hotel of the 1880's is another gross Victorian (classic) pile. Of more character, and set in the Friars' Hay district, a heavily, appropriately castellated fortress of 1890 is the Citadel of the Salvation Army. In the scholastic sphere Butterfield was the chosen designer when eventually there came the decision to resite Exeter School. There were also many commercial buildings of the nineteenth century; one at least of them, the offices (now bombed) of an insurance company in High Street, had considerable character as a work of Victorian Baroque. But nothing could have exceeded the distinctiveness, defying both classification and description but indelible in the memory, of the multi-galleried, liberally cubby-holed Deller's restaurant in Bedford Street. It was an essential part of a stop in Exeter till a high-explosive bomb removed it utterly from among the haunts of residents and travellers alike.

Chapter V

CREDITON

THE natural approach to Crediton from Exeter is across Cowley Bridge and so through Newton St. Cyres till one reaches the widely open valley of the Creedy, and nearer to the town the gate-lodges and parklands of the Bullers' Georgian mansion of Downes. But Crediton itself is as yet away from the traveller's gaze. It is pleasantly, remotely placed along both of the gentle, and then steeper slopes of a streamlet valley that runs down to the Creedy. It is invisible even from its own railway station, symbolic in its seclusion of the obscurity that has fallen upon it and upon the long-drawn splendour of its church since Leofric moved to Exeter with his bishop's throne. There can be few towns in England whose church is so magnificent and yet so little known.

The final journey is past some good pairs of late Georgian houses, past a site that may be that of the 1549 skirmish of Crediton barns, and so over the slight hill that conceals Crediton from the traffic arteries of the outer world. At once, in the eastern and lower part of the town, there stands the minster that ranks as Crediton's supremely important building. There are others of some minor note, and the Town Hall has a dignified Victorian classical façade, but to the minster church of Holy Cross, succeeding a Saxon cathedral and then for nearly five centuries a collegiate foundation hard by a great episcopal manor, the town of Crediton can show no rival (32).

The manor has disappeared, but there may, in a stone house in Dean Street (a significant name, though the head of the College was always called Precentor), and in a house called The Chantry, be some relics of the College buildings. If this be so they were separate from the church as were other late mediaeval college buildings like those at Westbury on Trym. But even within this field of church architecture there is little to divert us from the collegiate and now parochial church.

Its main feature, dominating all others and perhaps excessive in

88

32   Crediton: The Minster from the South-west

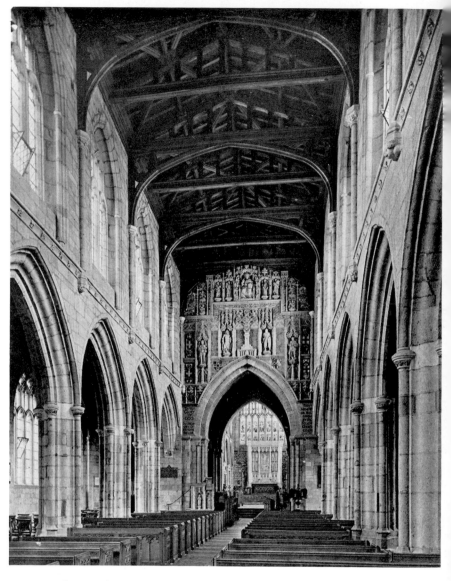

33 Crediton: The Nave and Crossing of the Minster, with the Choir beyond

relation to its other dimensions, is its great length; it exceeds Ottery in this respect, and also so famous a church as Bristol's St. Mary, Redcliffe. This length, at all events, in the eastern collegiate part of what was really a double church, may always have been above the average, for the Lady Chapel, projecting eastward and the feature that would make for such rare dimensions, was probably built as early as the later half of the thirteenth century.

There is nothing now to see of the structure, humble enough in all probability, that served for over a century as the Saxon cathedral. But the high status of a collegiate church continued to distinguish Crediton minster from those in the surrounding villages and country towns. In its structure, too, it soon had a feature by no means common in this remote and comparatively poor part of Devon. It was cruciform, with transepts and a central tower, before the twelfth century was out. The tower arches, slightly pointed but with simply scalloped capitals of a definitely Norman type, are the distinctive features remaining from this early period of the church's rebuilding; the lower part of the tower and the masonry of the two transepts came likewise from this late Norman phase. But it seems that in the next hundred years the collegiate church assumed its present remarkable and dignified plan.

I do not know what was the precise thirteenth-century lay-out of the college choir, but it seems certain, if one judges by what survives from that time, that it was of the generous size that befitted a foundation (of twelve prebends) considerable by non-cathedral standards. Nearness to Exeter, the presence in Crediton of an important bishop's manor, the memory of a past and more dignified status, all may have served to encourage architectural ambition. It may also be that in one important detail the eastern limb at Crediton was not, as at Ottery, a deliberate imitation of the architectural glories of Exeter, but an example to the designers of the Cathedral.

The Lady Chapel, projecting to the east of the choir, entered from the ends of the choir aisles by simple, dignified Early English arches, and flanked by the chapels that ended each aisle of the choir, is perhaps of a date not far from the middle years of the thirteenth century. The entrance arches, the canopied and gabled double piscina, the shafted arches of the inside of its windows, all these point to a date that cannot be much later than about 1260. More-over, the plan of this eastern terminal at Crediton, so closely similar to Bishop Bronescombe's ground plan for his Lady Chapel and its flanking chapels at Exeter, may perhaps have been a source of inspiration when the gradual rebuilding of the Cathedral was planned. For Crediton's east end not only resembles that at Exeter, it seems also to be the senior of the two as they stand today. It was here in the Lady Chapel that there occurred in 1315 an incident that impressed itself deeply on the chroniclers of the College. Bishop Stapledon of Exeter was saying Mass in the chapel when a blind man from Keynsham in Somerset, who had come two days earlier to Crediton and had there sojourned in the church, was suddenly restored to sight. The bishop made inquiries, and on being satisfied of a genuine miracle, gave orders for special thanksgivings.

What I do not know is whether the choir of Crediton church was also refashioned in the Early English style. One piece of building, however, makes it seem at least a likelihood. The block adjoining the south choir aisle contains in its three storeys rooms for the Treasury and a chapel, perhaps a vestry chapel, and is certainly in the thirteenth-century style. Being built to serve the needs of a collegiate church it is larger and more elaborate than such a building would have been in a simple parish church of the same time. It also corresponds, not in its details but in a general way, with the ground plan of the two-storeyed block containing St. James' chapel and a treasury that at Exeter fell victim to the direct bomb hit of 1942, the equivalent block surviving that runs off the choir's north aisle. So I do not think it past probability that this older collegiate foundation was a model for part of its successor's gradual rebuilding, even as at Ottery the plans of Grandisson were openly adapted from what he could see in his cathedral.

The rest of Crediton minster as we see it now is mostly early Perpendicular, the choir being rebuilt within older dimensions, the nave perhaps extended to meet the needs of a larger population. The thirteenth-century tower was given battlements and tall pinnacles in the Devon idiom one finds in such Dartmoor churches as Widecombe, Walkhampton, and Shaugh.

Choir and nave are much alike in their detail, five bays in the former, in the latter six; the choir clerestory has larger windows than that in the nave. There cannot have been many years between their rebuilding, and one may place them a little before 1400 or within the earliest years of the fifteenth century. Both are in a simple, dignified, not over-distinguished style; they belong without question to a church superior in status to most of the small parish churches in the county(33). Both are clerestoried and without triforium, and the same designer must surely have been responsible for nave and choir alike. But the nave, perhaps a little later than the choir, is slightly more ornate, with its carved corbels, and with its string-course of little rosettes that are executed in silvery-grey Beer stone. It appears that the nave was ripe for rebuilding in 1413 when Canon Langton of Exeter (we have noticed his brass in the Cathedral and his kinship to Bishop Stafford) left money for the work. Finally, at its western end, the church has the church's south porch and a great west window whose tracery, answering that of the window above the High Altar, proclaims a period when "Decorated" had not long given way to the more consistently vertical idiom of the succeeding style.

Such are the main architectural elements of this church that seems so strikingly large, as Southwell minster must have done before it became a cathedral, for so small a country town. Its size meant a great area of roofing over all its parts—nave, aisles, transepts and the like, and this roofing was covered with that metal that in its own time as now was so precious and exciting of covetousness. For when in 1545 the time came for the valuing of the college and for the taking of an inventory as a prelude to its dissolution, there was no commodity more carefully measured and valued than the lead of the roofs; the details given, both here and at Ottery, are a revealing sidelight on the cruder economic aspects of religious change. The Crediton lead, perhaps of high quality, for it was valued higher than at Ottery, was priced at £4 a ton; if one converts into the values of the 1950's the figure should be higher by thirty times or more.

So great a collegiate church should rightly be rich with its furnishings of the late Middle Ages. But not so Crediton. The stalls of the prebendaries have gone, and the interior saw many changes before the coming of the present stalls and reredos in the solidly correct Gothic of our own century's first decades. Late in the eighteenth century, when Polwhele wrote, there was an altarpiece, in obvious imitation of Archdeacon Hellyar's cathedral embellish- ment of 1639, which showed a "perspective view of a continuation of the church with figures of Moses and Aaron in front". But only the sadly smashed and broken sedilia survive of the late mediaeval choir fittings, and a piscina dates from about 1300. A simply designed Norman font recalls early parochial needs, and a badly worn pair of effigies, a knight in the armour of about 1390 and his lady beside him, are said to commemorate the centenarian Sir John de Sulley who died in 1387. Artistically more notable are Crediton's two monuments that fill two of the northern arches of the choir. One of them has a lawyer's effigy, that of Sir William Perriam (d. 1605), beneath a canopy whose decorated pilasters end in Ionic capitals. Sir William was one of the judges who finally condemned Mary Queen of Scots to her death at Fotheringhay. The other tomb, a more varied composition, with a broken pediment, four Ionic columns, and a lady's figure predominant over mere plaques to her husband and son, is twenty-five years later in the same century and recalls the important local family of the Tuckfields. Another Crediton celebrity, Sir Redvers Buller, is remembered by a scheme of decoration that covers all the nave's east wall above the western arch of the tower, an unhappy blend of Edwardian Gothic stonework and of colour rendered in profuse mosaic. Far more genuinely splendid, and a furnishing for which Crediton has no rival in England, is the superbly adorned chest of the late Middle Ages with its rich, flamboyant, traceried work and its carved panel that shows the Adoration of the Shepherds. It may have come from such a Continental district as Flanders, but whatever its origin it is a glorious treasure for the church to possess, as remarkable for the richness of its carving in wood as for the Lily of the Annuncia- tion and other delicate chasing that adorns the ironwork of its lock (11).

The market excepted, the rest of Crediton comes as something of an anticlimax after the scale and splendour of the minster. It is, of course, a busy little country town of about 4,000 people, the largest

place in the thinly populated forty miles between Exeter and Barnstaple, a place for marketing and shopping whose more recent
activities include the business of a manufacturing chemist. But the
successive fires have seen to it that the town's aspect is almost wholly
of the eighteenth century or from periods nearer still to our own
time, and to add to the impression of relative modernity the High
Cross was moved in 1758 from the foot of Bowden Hill. A little
way up the same hill the Bowden Hill Chapel, founded in 1688 and
now that of a Unitarian congregation, was rebuilt in 1729 as a
delightful piece of early Georgian Nonconformist architecture, with
admirable floral plasterwork above its pedimented main door. Then
along the town's main street there are some excellent Georgian
houses of various dates within a period between 1743 and about 1820,
most of them in red brick, and one, about two centuries old, much
dignified above its fellows by a pediment, a little cupola, and a bell.
From the street itself there climb at right angles a number of ancient
cobbled alleys that give Crediton its element of the "rambling
picturesque".

But the cream of Crediton's secular architecture is from the period
of the Greek Revival. The area that contains the market was laid
out in the 1830's under the auspices of the Bullers, and Market
Street has an excellent series of houses with balustrading and Ionic
doors. The market itself forms a balanced, well-planned group. At
one side is a monumental archway, at each end a pedimented gable
with Buller heraldry to adorn it, at each corner a truly admirable
composition that comprises in one cottage design a Regency shop
front and the chastely embellished windows of the shopkeeper's
house. The whole composition, constructed in an attractive, mellow
red brick, is not unworthy to stand for our judgment beside the
contemporary, though larger markets by Fowler of Exeter(10).

Chapter VI

OTTERY ST. MARY

THE site of Ottery gives it the makings of a rich, fertile, delightful manor, of a small town that could, for all its being off the main London to Exeter road and, in modern times,* away from the main line of railway from Waterloo, be something of a centre of manufacture and marketing for much of the rich agricultural district around it. But its real glory is more of a surprise, owing more to external factors and deliberate inspiration that have little to do with the placing of the town in the valley of the Otter, a stream entirely separate from the Exe, as it courses turgidly down from the Blackdown Hills to the English Channel. There are three factors above all others that make up the Ottery that is worth visiting today. They are the church, the factory, and Coleridge. The minster and its close surroundings, the precincts drastically altered since the late Middle Ages, and the whole scene considerably changed in modern times, must inevitably be the main subject of any chapter on the physical appearance of the town.

We have seen how the manor belonged, from Edward the Confessor's time and till Bishop Grandisson bought it, to the secular canons of Rouen Cathedral. But Ottery can show no Norman architecture; for the beginnings of what we now see we must turn to the thirteenth century and to the work of the years just before Bishop Bronescombe's time and early in his episcopate.

The size and wealth of the manor of Ottery were always above the average for the Devon countryside. It was likely that the village church should have been superior to many of its neighbours, and so indeed we find it to have been. For the shell of part of the parish church that Bishop Bronescombe consecrated in 1259 is still there to contain the work of transformation carried out by Grandisson, and of this thirteenth-century building (perhaps started about 1250) enough remains to prove that it was of considerable size and great dignity. It had aisles whose walls contain the shafted and hooded lancets of the Early English period; as late as the early seventeenth century, when Risdon compiled his *Survey of Devon*, these "little and low" windows were "so bedecked with the Armories of diverse Benefactors, more especially of the Founders, that instead of *Lux fiat*, it may be verified, that they are umbrated thereby" (the glass was probably of the fourteenth century, put in by Grandisson when he had founded the College). The breadth between these outer walls would have allowed for a spacious chancel. The nave, if ever it existed, seems mostly to have disappeared. There were also transepts, but we cannot tell if there was a central tower.

But when Bishop Grandisson, who was, to quote Risdon, "affected to the zealous liturgies of those times", came to found his college, the older church was inadequate in its dignity for his more ambitious requirements. He enlarged, recast, and refurnished it to suit the liturgical needs, with a special devotion to Our Lady, of his new foundation. The resulting minster, much altered by nineteenth-century restorers, and with much of its present Gothic decoration of their period, is for three reasons both a rare treasure of beauty and of the utmost interest to those who love our mediaeval architecture. Having left much of the earlier work in being, Grandisson and his designers seem to have felt themselves bound to model much of their fourteenth-century construction on existing Early English models; like the naves at Exeter and Westminster the minster at Ottery is in part a striking case of "archaism" in mediaeval art. Yet in so far as Grandisson's builders allowed themselves a clear field they evolved a decidedly unusual, "advanced" design that looked forward rather than back and was considerably more "progressive" than the bishop's nave at Exeter. Lastly, the plan at Ottery, and the liturgical arrangements at this newest of Devon's collegiate churches, were modelled with great exactness on what already existed at the Cathedral; the bishop's own guidance seems clearly responsible for the close correspondence.

What Grandisson did was to gut the whole of the "Bronescombe" chancel (and the nave if this existed), and while keeping the aisle walls, at least in the chancel, to build within the same breadth an entirely new vaulted structure. He also added the two double-storeyed vestry or treasury blocks, one off each choir aisle. In their functions they must have corresponded to the single addition made to the southern side of the choir at Crediton, but they helped at Ottery to produce a ground plan of the eastern limb that corresponds exactly to the chapel of St. James at Exeter and its unbombed opposite number off the north aisle of the cathedral choir. The additions made at Ottery would have provided the extra sacristy and storage space required by a college of secular canons.

It may be that the church as Grandisson left it had narrower aisles than before; it certainly had heavy stone vaulting which was strongly supported by the aisle roofs and reinforced by little founda-tion walls running to and fro beneath the floors. Indeed the whole structure has about it a feeling of sturdy solidity not wholly in tune with the delicacy and grace that were then the hallmark of fourteenth-century Gothic work; the impression is confirmed by that "archaism" which harks back so constantly to the simple "lancet" architecture of Bronescombe's time and before.

In architectural essentials, though not in all the details of their decoration, the choir and nave of Bishop Grandisson's two-purpose church are alike. The structural choir has six bays (one of them behind the altar screen), the nave has five. The aisles, vaulted by Grandisson in a simple manner to harmonise with the surviving lancets of the Early English chancel, are narrow and simple in design; their windows must be those that Risdon found darkened with armorial glass. But the nave and choir are at the same time more elaborate and architecturally less conservative than the outer work. The main arches are of simple architecture akin to that of early Perpendicular. There is no triforium, but in its stead a single canopied niche stands over the apex of every arch. The windows of the clerestory, simpler in their tracery than such windows would normally have been in the late 1330's, are comparatively small. There has, of course, been no attempt to eliminate the clerestory, and the niches above the arches pay tribute to the concept of the triforium, but the visual impression, particularly as one looks from due west to due east, is akin to that of a "single-storeyed" church like the contemporary, pioneering choir of St. Augustine's Abbey (now the cathedral) at Bristol(36). The pattern of the choir vault is also

34 Ottery: The Minster from the South-East

35 Exeter: St. Mary Arches

36 Ottery: The Nave and Choir of the Minster

not unlike that of the Bristol choir; in the nave it is simpler, without the cusps, the multiple ribbing, and the particularly beautiful bosses which in the choir show St. John the Baptist and scenes from the life of the Virgin. For the choir, its ornaments, and its eastward extension were specially given over to Grandisson's own devotion to the Mother of God; over the crossing a boss shows the bishop himself, and in the nave they are largely heraldic, a repetition of the Arms of Grandisson and Montacute, a pointer to joint financing of the church by the bishop and his sister the Countess of Salisbury.

Of the choir's furnishings, many of them perhaps far richer and more detailed than the main outlines of the building, there is sadly little that has survived the post-Reformation centuries and the scourings out by Butterfield in one of his less happy phases (his restoration was begun in 1849). The stalls, essential, distinctive furnishings of a collegiate or monastic choir, were not in fact designed to any very elaborate pattern and may not have had canopies. Some are now in the Lady Chapel, some remain in the choir; the simple misericord carvings are heads or else shields of the Grandisson Arms. The sanctuary has lovely canopied sedilia, the Easter Sepulchre, built in the manner of an altar tomb, is now the substructure of an Elizabethan monument. But the whole proportion of the collegiate choir in Grandisson's double church was altered by Butterfield. The floor of the whole east end, choir, crossing, and transepts alike, had originally been raised a few feet above that of the nave. The choir with its stalls had itself been shut off from the rest of the building by a screen whose design may have closely followed that of Bishop Stapledon's newly-built screen at Exeter. This choir screen had accommodated the boys of the Grammar School as late as Parson Coleridge's time, and it seems likely that it perished at the hands of restorers earlier than Butterfield. He, however, was the designer who completed the liturgically awkward process whereby a double church designed for the separate worship of canons and laity was thrown open as an elongated parochial church. The floor of the transepts and of the western part of the choir was brought down to the level prevailing in the nave. With the church thus opened out, a fine, if somewhat distant view was now given of what must have been the most glorious feature of the choir provided for the canons—the altar screen; above it is a row of little canopied niches which may, according to Canon Dalton, be the surviving heads of a septet of lancets in the east wall of the thirteenth-century chancel. The altar screen's niches and canopies of Grandisson's time were scraped away at the Reformation to make a flat surface for the Commandments and Royal Arms; the niches we now see are a restoration, not without credit and beauty, by Blore in 1833. For Butterfield's was not the only work done on Ottery minster in the nineteenth century. So fine a building attracted many eminent consultants, so that Rickman, Woodyer of Guildford, Blore, and Butterfield all came to give advice or actually to execute the rechiselled and polychromed building now available to the parish. But a glorious fourteenth-century survival, lofty, heraldic, undefaced, is the reredos' armorial cornice with its ten shields that bear record of the branches, lay and episcopal, of the Grandisson family, of some of their splendid alliances (Montacute and Mortimer among them), of Courtenay, of the Royal Family under Edward III; the quartering of France "ancient" with England is a proof that the work, probably one of the last items in the church's re-equipment, was done a little later than 1339. No doubt this flattery of Royalty from so highly connected a bishop was as deliberate as the inclusion in the College's dedication of St. Edward the Confessor, the name-saint and patron of the King.

The nave, for all its Grandisson and Montacute heraldry, is less elaborate than the choir must have been, the vaulting is simpler, and the effective arcading at its western end is not original, but a modern version of that on the back of the altar screen. The western entrance has, however, a degree of exterior magnificence with its twin doorways and flanking niches. I will speak later of the nave's excellent Grandisson monuments, but for the final architectural item in the bishop's *Frauenkirche* we must go eastwards to that feature so rare in purely parochial churches, yet so natural in a collegiate or monastic foundation, the Lady Chapel that runs eastwards, with little chapels on each side of it to flank its western part, exactly in the manner of the Cathedral. Crediton, Exeter, Ottery, the sequence of similar eastern terminals was now complete.

Here, too, is an "archaism" of style. The east window, of seven lights and put in at a date late enough for it to have had Decorated tracery as elaborate as that in the Cathedral nave, in fact has no tracery at all and may in its simplicity perpetuate the window design of the church consecrated in 1259. The outer wall is more elaborate, for here is a set of beautifully canopied niches. The vaulting of this chapel is simple, but two of its corbels are the most important in the church. For here, in the chapel set aside for the Offices of Our Lady which were his special delight, is Bishop Grandisson's head, and opposite to it the head of a lady who seems likely to be his sister the Countess of Salisbury. The corbels *may* be portraits; the bishop's shows a dignified ecclesiastic in early middle age (Grandisson was forty-five when he founded the College), the lady's does not belie Catherine Grandisson's reputation for the beauty which is said to have entranced the young Edward III.

The Lady Chapel, unlike the choir, has kept its much restored screen that at one time supported a pair of small organs for the accompaniment of the chants(37). Its three arches, with their beautiful cusping, call strongly to mind Bishop Stapledon's choir screen in the Cathedral. Within are some of the stalls from the choir arranged now as the mediaeval seating might have been in the Lady Chapel itself. The wooden eagle lectern is a veteran of its own species; Canon Dalton suggests that it may first of all have done duty for the reading of the Gospel of the Mass from the main screen of the choir. Conspicuous also within the Lady Chapel are Butter-field's restorations (or rather reproductions) of the sculptured con-secration crosses that survive, though greatly worn away, around the church's exterior; they are one of Ottery's most unusual survivals.

So much for the main elements, nave, choir, and Lady Chapel, of the collegiate-cum-parochial church as Grandisson saw it finished by about 1342. But the most remarkable of all its debts to Exeter has yet to be described. Alone of all our non-episcopal churches (albeit it owed almost everything to a distinguished prelate) the church at Ottery directly copies Exeter with its flanking, transeptal towers(34). The process of conversion was exactly the reverse of what had recently happened at Exeter. There the two Norman towers were opened out as transepts; at Ottery the thirteenth-century transepts were unroofed and carried up as a pair of low, solid towers. Their "archaism" is as pronounced as elsewhere in the church, for the upper windows, though of fourteenth-century date, are of Early English type, and the shallow recesses for the transept altars were given sets of five lancets apiece and outside gables in a way reminiscent of those at the famous cruciform Berkshire church of Uffington. The transepts were vaulted by Grandisson (the central boss of the crossing shows the bishop), and in the southern one the mediaeval orrery clock is yet another striking parallel with the collegiate Cathedral of Exeter. There could scarcely have been a church so closely and deliberately modelled on the Cathedral of its diocese, in its structure as also in the statutes for its worship and corporate life, as this beautiful offering of the mediaeval aristocracy at a time when feudal chivalry was at its most splendid.

This aristocratic flavour remained about Ottery till the very end of its pre-Reformation history. The population of the parish may well have grown, along with that in such towns as Cullompton and Tiverton, as the cloth trade developed in East Devon. But when the time came at Ottery for more church accommodation for worship-ping parishioners, that space was provided, not by Ottery's com-mercial equivalent of Cullompton's Lane or Tiverton's Greenway, but by a great lady whose social standing was hardly less than that of the Princess Catherine in Tiverton Castle. The outer north aisle at Ottery is particularly good as a specimen of fan-vaulted late Perpendicular architecture; along with its north porch it formed a noble addition to the nave and must have greatly helped the worship of the local laity. Its design, in particular the plan of its six-light west window and the panelling and pendents of its fan vault (46), make it seem certain that this aisle was designed by the same hand as the Lane aisle at Cullompton, just as the Cullompton ship carvings must surely be by the same craftsmen that did Greenway's ships at Tiverton. But the aisle at Ottery, a little simpler in its details than the work at Cullompton, relies largely on heraldry for its decoration though the capitals of its pillars have among their carving much foliage, grotesques, and the head of a charming elephant (5). The heraldry of the aisle is, however, all-important; it gives a partial clue to the immense distinction of the high-born lady in the Midlands who paid for the work.

The builder of the "Dorset" aisle (the structure is misnamed, for she was probably Countess of Wiltshire at the time of its erection) was born Cicely Bonville, the daughter of William Bonville, Lord Harington; she was a distant descendant of Bishop Grandisson's sister, the Countess of Salisbury. The deaths, in many cases in battle (as Yorkists) or by execution during the Wars of the Roses, of many of her male relatives, made her the heiress in her own right to many East Devon estates, both in Ottery parish and elsewhere; we find that though she lived away from Devon she also added an aisle to the nave of the church at Axminster. Through her mother she was a great-great-granddaughter of Edward III, and also a niece to Warwick the Kingmaker. Her first marriage, to Thomas Grey, Marquis of Dorset, Baron Ferrers, and Baron Astley, gave her a royal mother-in-law, for Elizabeth Grey, who had been wife to her husband's father, became Queen Elizabeth Woodville after her first husband had died at the second battle of St. Alban's. By this same alliance she also became great-grandmother to Lady Jane Grey. Her second husband, whom she married in her forties, in 1503, was of equal, and for himself of dangerous distinction. He was Henry Stafford (hence the Stafford knots on the aisle at Ottery), younger son of the second Duke of Buckingham and brother to Edward, third Duke of Buckingham whose royal blood, combined as was that of the young Marquis of Exeter with an unwise parade (at Thornbury Castle in Gloucestershire) of worldly pomp, proved as fatal to him in 1521 as Henry Courtenay's similar unwisdom did in Henry VIII's equally unmerciful later years. But the Earl of Wiltshire (as he had become in 1510) escaped the king's dangerous attentions; he and his Countess Cicely were childless and that may have made their lives safer. The Earl died in 1523 and his widow in 1530, she being buried in the Warwickshire collegiate church of Astley where she had founded a chantry. Yet it seems, from the owl of Bishop Oldham that appears on two of the aisle's capitals, that by 1519 she had started this last, and not least, glorious architectural addition to the noblest of west-country collegiate churches.* The

* Veysey's Arms imply completion after 1519.

minster's history closes, as it had long persisted, on a note of uncompromising aristocracy.

The mediaeval tombs at Ottery number only two, a similar, distinguished pair that are placed under opposite arches in the nave. They are those of a younger brother of the bishop, Sir Otho de Grandisson who died in 1358-9, and of Beatrix his wife. The knight's figure has the armour of the fourteenth century's middle decades and his effigy, with its living posture and feeling of slightly restless movement, seems likely to be a product of the school of carvers that worked on the western image screen of Exeter Cathedral. More notable still is the pair of graceful ogee canopies with their cusping, their carving of rich foliage, and their shields as a course round the arches and in the spandrels (this last little detail recalls the Percy tomb in Beverley Minster). We have it from Risdon, who wrote within a century of the College's fall, that both of these tombs once had their shields "fairly adorned with coat armories, both now defaced by time" (38).

One turns in the end to the tombs and furnishings that are not of the Middle Ages. One of them is the mural monument, with its slightly crude classical design and fine standing figure of a man in the armour of the early seventeenth century, that commemorates a Coke of Thorne, who died in 1632. A canopy and pediment, of Elizabethan date and to John Haydon of Cadhay (d. 1587) are raised in the sanctuary above the structure of the older Easter Sepulchre. A far later mural monument is by the elder Bacon and is dated 1794, and there are somewhat earlier mural tablets to the family of the Vaughans. The same early Georgian period, to be precise the year 1722, gave us the magnificent pulpit of carved wood, a work that is altogether outstanding of its kind. For it is wholly Baroque in feeling with its admirable figures of the Evangelists; the maker was William Culne, a carver-carpenter of Ottery itself. Along with some early Tudor benches in the "Dorset" aisle, this pulpit is the one furnishing of note or beauty that Ottery minster now possesses. The other end of the scale of taste is surely touched by Butterfield's font, a square, ponderous composition of multi-coloured, geometrical marble, its cover of wood a bizarre essay in Rhineland Romanesque. There are also important monuments, for the most part of our own time, to the distinguished members of the Coleridge family.

Though remains of its collegiate buildings are still in the vicarage, and though Paternoster Row reminds us of the religious history of this part of Ottery, the church stands now for the most part on its own, with little in its surroundings to recall that here in the Middle Ages was a complete reproduction, on a smaller scale, of the pre´ cincts of a cathedral foundation. The Manor House to the north of the minster was where the Manor Courts were held, for the College was local landlord as well as being the leading religious establish´ ment of the district. To the south and west, in ordered succession and with little of the piecemeal, somewhat haphazard process of growth that slowly produced the Close at Exeter, there were grouped the buildings of the College; unlike those performing similar func´ tions in the cathedral city of Devon they were built to one original plan, most of them in all probability within a short initial period after 1337, the products of planning by the single, vigorous, un´ usually orderly mind of Bishop Grandisson. An octagonal Chapter House, cloisters, and a gatehouse lay south of the church; the library was a separate building and had six small windows, in the manner of such rooms, to light the intervals between the cases which held many books bequeathed by Grandisson himself. There were hospices, all built in the early days of the College, for the choristers, for the clerks, and for the "secondaries" who supported the chanting of the canons in choir. A schoolhouse for the choristers did lengthy duty in post´Reformation days as Ottery Grammar School. There were separate houses for the Warden, Precentor, Sacrist, and for the other canons; a house for the priest´vicars presupposed, as did Calendarhay at Exeter, that not all those on the foundation would always be resident. The cemetery of the College lay west of the church, between its nave and the row of canons' houses that bordered the Close. The scene was all of that order and detailed regulation that Grandisson so loved. The town and its laity, of course, existed, but they and their less carefully ordered life and worship were here relegated to a subordinate place. So then the régime at Ottery persisted, outlasting the monasteries and coming to within two years of Henry VIII's decease. Then at last the

commissioners and takers of inventories came as a prelude to dissolution. As at Crediton they numbered the vestments and plate and put
a price on the carefully measured, deeply prized lead on the church's
roofs—at 53s. 4d. a ton it was cheaper than the £4 value they had
placed on the newer, and presumably better conditioned lead at
Crediton. But we may be thankful, in both places, that a better
fate awaited the two minsters than to become quarries and builders'
yards or a source of the military stores then needed for Henry's
conduct of an Anglo-French war.

Its minster and its link with Coleridge are alone enough to
make Ottery supremely worth a visit. It is as well, for the town has
little enough in its buildings to distinguish it; demolitions and fires
have both in large measure deprived it of character and charm.
There are indeed some pleasant little Georgian houses round the
east and north of the churchyard, the plaque to Coleridge is to the
south of it, and Paternoster Row* and Cornhill come as interesting
parallels to the street naming of the City of London.

But the best of Ottery's domestic building is in Broad Street.
Colby House is Georgian of the middle period, Raleigh House
belongs obviously to the Exeter school of late eighteenth-century
housebuilding in brick with trickings-out in Coade stone. The
Wesley Chapel has the date 1829 in its round-headed gable; lower
down the street one draws nearer to the river, the railway, and East
Devon's greatest relic, since Heathcoat's Tiverton factory was burnt,
of early factory industrialism.

The Factory, as Thackeray calls it in *Pendennis* (with Ottery
featured as Clavering St. Mary) is of great social interest as well as
being an architectural adornment to the town. By the 1790's the old
domestic system of the West of England cloth industry was yielding
to mills, at first only for the finishing of cloth that had been woven
in the weavers' homes, then as time went on for the weaving and
finishing processes alike. In 1788 a scheme was set afoot for the
building on the outskirts of Ottery of a great serge factory that might
do for declining Ottery what the great new factory was soon to do
for Tiverton. By 1790 a sum of £40,000 had been found, and the
still surviving factory was built by two local capitalists who were

* Where Dr. Pevsner has noted rainwater heads of 1759 and 1778.

37 The Lady Chapel
Screen (Lectern and
Sedilia beyond)

38   The Tomb of Sir Otho
de Grandisson, d. 1359

39 Fore Street, A Mansion of *c.* 1740

40 St. George's, 1714–30

prominent in the woollen and banking trade; they were John Duntze of Exeter, and Sir George Yonge who was also in Parliament and was Secretary of State for War in 1789. They may well have employed as their designer the same William Gream of Ottery who, in another few years, designed the great Tiverton mill; their water wheel was the largest in Britain. But their new building was not long on woollens. It was a silk factory in 1823 and now it has settled down, almost unaltered in its external aspect, as the workshop of a light engineering concern. It is a fine brick building, of five storeys and of a gaunt yet dignified rectangular simplicity, a splendid specimen within its own comparatively unappreciated architectural field. Its more distinctive features are its gate-posts and its classical front door that come as a pointer to its late Georgian date.

Chapter VII

TIVERTON

THERE could be no more beautiful, nor more obvious a site for a town than that of Tiverton. By Devon standards the place is of fair size; it has in fact passed through varying phases of relative importance in the county. At one time, with its cloth trade at its peak, it was among Devon's leaders in point of population. For it had nearly 9,000 people in the early years of George I, but during the rest of the eighteenth century the figures fluctuated at lower levels. At the end of the century there were hardly more than 7,000; now there are about another 4,000. But only the growth in Devon of such large seaside resorts as Exmouth, Paignton, and Torquay has put Tiverton back to the secondary position in the county which it held in its earliest days.

The Exe valley does not, above its confluence with the Culm, in the broad valley country near Brampford Speke, afford many points where a town of importance might reasonably grow up. The one obvious locality for such developments is the neighbourhood of Tiverton. For there, at the place of the Two Fords over the Exe and the Lowman, another tract of spacious and fruitful valley country intervenes between two reaches of the Exe where the river runs turbulently, and in the manner of a moor-born stream, between lofty, steep, and wooded hills. A fortress at such a point could be the key to the valley of the upper Exe; a town could be the economic centre of a wide area of tilth and pasture. The gentle, easy, spacious valley of the Lowman leads direct towards Taunton and the more distant goal of London; it was by this approach that modern transport first reached Tiverton about 1810 in the shape of the Grand Western Canal, and later with the railway from its junction on the main line of the "Bristol and Exeter". Such was the general setting provided for the town by the unchanging aspects of geology. The more immediate outlines of rock and river imposed the exact historic location of Tiverton.

For between the two rivers a ridge of rising rocky ground runs down to a triangular point; at the top end of that rough triangle the Exe sweeps down on one side in such a way as to leave a steeply sloping bank some fifty feet high. Upon this eminence the castle was naturally placed. The church of St. Peter, the chief place of worship of a large, populous parish which contained many dependent chapels, arose near the castle. The town, as it grew up, was first placed within the area between the rivers, and then, as the cloth industry greatly increased and as water power was made copiously available by leats run off from the Exe, a section of it devoted mainly to industry developed, as in the similarly placed areas of Exeter, in the low-lying area by Tiverton's principal river. In our own time, of course, the town has spread considerably outside its earlier limits.

The town has its two main lines of railway approach, one from Tiverton Junction on the line to London, the other direct from Exeter up the Exe valley. There is also the disused yet still water-filled course of the canal. In summer the area of the canal port is a charming scene, with waterlilies to adorn it as the last stretch of the waterway broadens out into a basin whose edging and facing of worked stone still survive. More immediate access is by the three bridges, two of them over the Lowman, the chief one carrying the Exeter road over the more impressive stream of the Exe. It was a structure of stone from at least as early as the reign of Elizabeth I. As the chief means of access to a growing commercial town it was constantly in use, was widened in 1802 and again, with the building of its present balustrade, in 1818. It is not one of Tiverton's more impressive pieces of building, nor would it be easy, except from a boat on the river, to appreciate its qualities did they happen to be nearer to those of James Green's masterpiece at Cowley. The Lowman bridges are also unexciting. The one at the bottom of St. Andrew's Street is of the eighteenth century, with one major arch and two small pointed ones in an earlier manner. The principal bridge, close to Old Blundell's, has its three arches of the 1770's, but these are overlaid and almost invisible beneath later rebuilding.

From the Exe bridge it is best to go straight through the western side of old Tiverton, and so past the parish church to the castle that still in large measure survives on its eminence that peers so strikingly above the bend in the Exe. It is a castle surprisingly unknown, for relatively to its ancient state it has more to see than has Rougemont at Exeter; the remoter situation of Tiverton itself, and the fact that the castle has not normally been open, may well be the chief cause of this relative obscurity.

For all its twelfth-century origin, Tiverton Castle can show no Norman work, and its centre is now to a large extent filled by a dwelling-house of the eighteenth century . North of that house there may once have been the motte and round tower of an earlier, Norman, castle. But all of what we see now is of the Courtenay period and later, with no features that one can place earlier than the fourteenth century.

The castle of the late Middle Ages was roughly square, and seemingly without any keep or dominant tower; its military architecture was of Plantagenet and not of Norman character. Three of its corner towers were round, and of these the one at the south-east survives impressively to confront the visitor as he passes the churchyard. As a military obstacle the western side must always have been the most forbidding as it crowned the steep riverward slope; between its two towers there was a projecting turret of square plan, but of this and of the round tower to the north-west there are only the lower courses. On the northern side and at the north-east corner there are no survivals, only a well-stocked kitchen garden that spreads over their site. The sides of the castle had moats whose water was found from the Countess Isabella's Town Leat, benevolence to the townsmen and security for herself being both allowed for in ample measure by the copiousness of her artificial stream. The portions of the castle of which much remains are the southern and eastern sides of what was once a wide inner courtyard.

The Hall, and perhaps a chapel to the west of it, lay along most of the southern side. Of its distinguishing features there remain some "Decorated" windows of two lights; below them are roughly constructed gun ports of Tudor times. West of the Hall the castle's south-west tower contained the "solar" and other living apartments leading away from the Hall. It was not rounded like the others, but was built square to allow more spacious quarters for its owners. A fireplace is still to be seen that must have warmed an upper room, and one of the windows, with "Decorated" tracery in its upper part, is "advanced" in its plan in that it has a transom and below it a window design of sturdy, utilitarian type, curved at the start, but then square-headed, that one finds in early mediaeval doorways of domestic or secular nature. The window may be contemporary with Ottery choir or with the early transoms in the choir of Bristol Cathedral; the work as a whole seems to be from the time of Hugh Courtenay, the Earl of Devon who died in 1340.

The main gate is beneath an eastward projecting tower; it seems to date, in its enlarged and embellished state, from the fifteenth century. Its vaulted gate passage is excellent work, and the rosettes that decorate its outer arch betoken a period of greater delicacy and refinement in such aspects of domestic building.

Tiverton Castle must have been at its best in the last years of the Middle Ages, not in the front rank of castles or so grand a piece of military architecture as some, not the Courtenays' only home but good enough to be the residence of the Dowager Countess who was also a Princess. With the fall of the Courtenays came the beginning of decay. Its domestic centre moved from the hall range to the reconstructed block on the eastern side, and the square-headed, mullioned windows imply new domestic work in the later Tudor decades. As a residence the castle now became more modest, and the decay of its fortified parts was probably swifter after its final capture in the Civil War. Within the walls, and abutting on the Tudor eastern range, is the house built about 1700 by Peter West. It has the curved, projecting cornice of its period, and within there is a noble staircase with baluster rails. Projecting into the courtyard is a dignified porch, its brickwork a diaper of red and dark blue that we shall also encounter at Cullompton. Final touches are the fireplaces in the Adam taste, and outside the main enclosure a house and lodge, in the "churchwarden" Gothic of about 1800, lie close to the castle walls. Tiverton Castle may have decayed far below its mediaeval dignity, yet it still provides an assortment and an epitome of our building history.

The "civic" or "sovereign" buildings of Tiverton are a sad anti-climax after the interest and merit of the castle.

There seems to have been no Town Hall in the Middle Ages. Nor, in the absence of a corporation, does there seem to have been much need for such a building. So when in 1615 a Charter of Incorporation was given to the town, the "Town House" was built on the site of the desecrated chapel of St. George; it may have been fashioned out of its actual structure. Many changes had been made by 1788, and according to Dunsford (in 1790) the building was then a cramped jumble of Court House, Prison, Mayor's Parlour, dwelling-house, cellarage, and local bank. It may have been picturesque, and in portions "elegant", but no doubt it was soon found inconvenient in a modern town and did not survive the Victorian Age. The present Town Hall, not an ornament to Tiverton, is of the 1860's and had one Lloyd of Bristol as its architect. Far better, and placed half-way down St. Andrew's Street, is the admirably proportioned, dignified, Grecian Bridewell of 1844-5. I do not know who was its designer, but he did well for Tiverton with his excellent stone front and its tall, monumental, recessed arch with its impressively heavy cornice above(42). At the other end of the town the workhouse is a typically well proportioned design of the 1830's, and was an early work of Gilbert Scott. It replaced a large set of brick and stone buildings of 1704 whose authorising Act was one of the early ones for such institutions, being passed in 1698. The name of its designer, John Abbot, is the first architect's name of which we hear in Tiverton. It is clear, from Dunsford's detailed account, that this workhouse was a really important, carefully contrived building, specially designed for its purpose (unlike the famous St. Peter's Hospital at Bristol) and thus of pioneering social importance. The seal of the Corporation, thoughtfully provided by a Mr. Gwynn, was the representation of an ant-hill!

There was no mediaeval monastery or other religious house in Tiverton. But the parish was unusually large, spreading out into the surrounding hamlets and containing outlying chapels as well as the central place of worship in the actual town. It was not the only such parish in the district; Crediton and Cullompton were others whose early mediaeval organisation was on the same pattern. One rector was too few for such a commitment, so the churches

were served on a "collegiate" system of several priests, each one provided for by the tithes of a portion of the land. At Crediton the
system was in time given the formal, liturgical recognition of a
collegiate, or minster church. At Cullompton we shall see how it
disappeared. But at Tiverton the system of four separate rectors,
with their "portions" of Clare, Prior's, Pitt, and Tidcome, lasted
as late as 1889, when Bishop Temple abolished it. The rectors in
turn did duty in St. Peter's; they and their curates had also the care
of the outlying chapels. But of this "college" history of Tiverton
parish no trace can be seen in the architecture of St. Peter's, the
chancel being small and in no way like the minster choirs of Crediton
and Ottery. Nor, with one exception, has St. Peter's any architectural relics of the early Middle Ages. Its aspect is that of a great
town church of the Perpendicular period, its idiom and decoration
it owes mainly to the commercial middle class and only slightly to
the lords of the adjacent castle.

The one Norman relic, reset in a wall that was rebuilt a century
ago, is the small north doorway, adorned with continuous zigzag
moulding and leading towards the castle and its postern gate. The
whole of the rest is Perpendicular, some of it from fairly early in
the fifteenth century, some from the early, pre-Reformation, Tudor
decades, much of it by way of Victorian restoration and enlargement.

By 1530 St. Peter's was one of the most spacious parochial
churches in Devon. Of the work surviving from the late Middle
Ages the most dignified feature is the west tower. To its parapet it
is about 100 feet high, the battlements were rebuilt in 1673, the
buttresses have grotesque little beasts perched riskily on the sloping
"set offs" that mark the points where they lessen in thickness. The
pinnacles are simple in design and less ambitious than those at
Cullompton, but the kinship of the two towers, as also their
affinity to that at Broad Clyst near Exeter, is amply apparent from a
perceptive glance.

The arches from the chancel to its chapels may date from early in
the fifteenth century, but those in the rest of the church, with
canopied niches on their pillars and good carved capitals, were
originally set up in the late Perpendicular period about 1500. Each
of the nave arcades has six arches, and above them was a clerestory,

repeated in the rebuilding that started in 1853. This clerestory, a rarity in Devon, lent distinction and dignity to a church that came nearer than most in the county to the stately fashion followed by the church builders of fifteenth-century Somerset(50).

But as they stand today the arches in St. Peter's, in shape and design a copy of those that stood for over three centuries, are a curious colour mixture, the creamy yellow of Bath stone used by the Victorian rebuilders, the capitals preserved from the older work and delicately silver in their stone from Beer. The subjects are varied; the capitals on the north are perhaps the older set with their merchants' marks, foliage, birds, angels, and Courtenay heraldry. The capitals on the south bear Greenway's monogram and the badges of the Tudors; the aisle itself was widened by Greenway and we shall see how he copiously adorned it. But the chancel arch, panelled and of lofty dignity, is again a reminder of the Courtenays. For high upon each side are the eagle and sheaf of sticks that were their family badge, and their arms, *or three torteaux*, are surrounded with the Garter for Edward Courtenay, K.G., holder of the Devon earldom from 1485 to 1509.

Such then, Greenway's final embellishments excluded, is the main structure of St. Peter's after the numerous changes in its history. One misses, of course, many things that at one time or another have beautified the building. Worst of all the losses is the Courtenay chapel. It stood to the north of the main fabric; it is not finally clear whether it was a separate building or in some way connected to the north aisle. Its monuments, especially that of the Princess Catherine, are likely to have been splendid. The screen and its loft are gone bar a few of the lower panels; it had many vicissitudes, for the organ of 1696 was first set upon it as an eastern terminal to an "auditory" nave. Then from 1813 it carried a gallery for the children of the charity schools; another for the Blundell's boys was more obscurely over the south door. The roofing of the church has often changed, for the 1770's and 1780's gave roofs "of the Doric order" (Dunsford) to one of the aisles and to the nave. The nave roof in its turn made way, about 1820–4, for a bossed vault of plaster in the fifteenth-century manner; at the same time the Queen Anne seats for the Mayor and Corporation were sadly taken away, though the

41 St. Paul Street and Church (by Manners and Gill, of Bath, 1854–6)

42 The Prison, 1844–6

TIVERTON TOWNSCAPE

43   Tiverton: Greenway's Chapel

44   Cullompton: Lane's Aisle

THE EAST DEVON CLOTHIERS, 1520–30

Mayor's lion and unicorn are still in the church. The Jacobean altar rails are no more, and the splendid canopied pulpit of Bishop Cotton's time (1598–1621) has a Victorian successor.

The most famous work in Tiverton Church is that which Green-way put into it and finished about 1517. His south aisle and chapel are part of that movement to enlarge and adorn which simultaneously caused additions of such note, and almost certainly with the same designers, at Ottery, Tiverton, and Cullompton. For the aisles of all three churches have in their end-walls the six-light windows of similar design, and though Greenway's enlarged south aisle at Tiverton has none of the delicate fan vaulting of Ottery and Cullompton, the exterior details on both of the merchants' churches are clearly copied one from the other, with Tiverton perhaps the senior of the two.

The keynote of Greenway's new work was a somewhat vulgar profusion of ornament. The buttresses of his main aisle he encrusted with a medley of woolpacks, trade-marks, anchors, and ships of the time; above the buttresses the whole parapet and its battlements are unusually elaborate. But the most concentrated decoration, as much a *tour de force* as the completely carved granite exterior of the contemporary church at Launceston, was reserved for the south porch and for Greenway's projecting chantry chapel of two bays (43). The chapel, like the aisle, has an ornate parapet, but between it and the window stage, the latter itself being enriched with panelling and ships' anchors, we have two layers of adornment, themselves divided by a cornice with little sculptured groups from the life of Christ. The upper cornice has heraldry, of Henry VIII, of Greenway (his initials, too, are liberally scattered about the church), of the London Companies of the Drapers and Merchant Adventurers to which he belonged. The lower belt of carving repeats the buttresses with a row of varied ships. Some have one mast, others three (4), some are cargo carriers, others perhaps the warships of their time. They and many other features of the church's outside carving are terribly worn, but these ships remain as a valuable, though not unique, nautical record in stone, a tribute to the vehicles of Greenway's wealth. Within, the chapel, now furnished again, has little of its old magnificence, for its stone screen has gone and the panelling and pendents of its ceilings are not Tudor work. But the figures of John and Joan Greenway survive from their brass, of nearly life size and outstanding among the civilian brasses of their time. They and the main design of the chapel are parts of a Gothic conception, but the chapel's most refined feature is the delicate early Renaissance detail of the oaken door dividing the chapel from the south porch. The porch itself was also Greenway's work, and then in 1825 it was pulled down and re-erected along the old lines. It retains much of its Tudor detail, not least the Arms of the Princess Catherine in the place of honour. A sculpture of the Assumption, the Greenways kneeling on either side in veneration, is over the church's main door.

The monuments and furnishing in St. Peter's have an interest of their own. The best of the chancel monuments is a table-tomb with Renaissance detail to the wool merchant John Waldron, who died in 1579, and one with crude caryatids at its corners that commemorates George Slee who died in 1613; his wife was a niece of Peter Blundell, and he, too, was a notable benefactor to Tiverton. Both of these table-tombs are basically mediaeval in design, but other monuments are more fully in the Renaissance tradition. There are some murals to the leading official and clerical family of the Newtes, while some in a more fully Baroque manner commemorate members of the Tiverton clothier and merchant community. Nor are these the only contemporary adornments of St. Peter's. The Renaissance organ case is of 1696 and the organ may have been by Bernhard Schmidt: it first stood in greater dignity on the screen, and the *putti* who once held up its surmounting mitres now languish aside in the church library. Another divorce has been that of the brass chandelier of 1707 from its splendidly decorative ironwork.

The early eighteenth century also saw the erection of the Chapel of Ease of St. George. In a town of much Nonconformity it was part of the Anglican campaign, started under Queen Anne and notably productive in London, to provide new churches in the towns. St. George's was started in 1714, its rainwater heads bear the date 1717, and it was not finished till 1730. I do not know its architect's name, but he gave Tiverton the best Georgian church in Devon. The outside, having no steeple, is no more than competent and gives little hint of the excellence within. There are good doorways, pediments over the slightly projecting east and west ends, and tiers of windows to light the ground and gallery floors. The inside is a reminiscence of Wren, five galleried bays with a shallow sanctuary and above it a panelled ceiling. The barrel vault has stone Ionic columns to support it; in harmony with them the sanctuary panelling is also Ionic and good rails enclose three sides of the altar (40).

St. Paul's in Westexe, with its tower and spire, is a Gothic achievement of the 1850's by the Bath designers Manners and Gill. Of the Nonconformist churches I have only noticed one of surviving merit. In St. Peter Street the Methodist Chapel of 1814 has a pedimented front that peers above a later portico in brick and stone.

Three of Tiverton's almshouses were founded by the town's important men in the wool and cloth trade of Tudor times. Greenway's is in Gold Street, the early sixteenth-century fabric much altered, but in a part of the founder's own time. The design of the chapel, and the nature of the carving and decoration, make it seem, as one would naturally expect, that the building was the work of the same school of craftsmen as worked on the chantry and porch of St. Peter's. More remarkable in its way is John Waldron's almshouse in Westexe; we are told that it was still being built in 1579 when its founder died. For here, despite an Elizabethan date, is a building closely modelled on what Greenway had commissioned. In front it has shallow-arched doorways and a loggia of timber, at its west end a little Perpendicular chapel in obvious imitation of that at Greenway's almshouse. Its tracery and the style of lettering recall the early decades of the century, and here, too, are the ship carvings as one has them at St. Peter's and at Cullompton. Slee's, the third of the almshouses, is of the early seventeenth century, standing in considerably restored condition, with its wooden galleries, at the bottom of St. Peter Street.

More famous, as one can tell from the history of Tiverton, and indeed from that of education as a whole, is Blundell's. Of the school's history I have spoken elsewhere; that history is itself largely embodied in the two sets of buildings, one Jacobean, one Victorian, that belong to the school.

Blundell died in 1601 and the old building was finished in another three years. Its site did not prove ideal, and to modern eyes seems cramped and inadequate, but in its own time the building was advanced and splendid among such places of learning. Being built for its own purpose and not fitted up (as Bristol Grammar School had been) in older buildings it matched the lavish provisions of Blundell's foundation. In its design it was reminiscent of a doubly transepted barn, and still more of an old-style manor with a long, spacious hall. The exterior, with its good masonry, its two projecting porches with their shell-headed niches, and three short wings running out at the back, is little changed since the early days, though alterations have been made at the riverward end, while the buttresses have been added and the mullioned windows lowered (49). The masonry, by the school's own custom, has been engraved wholesale with the names of pupils. Blackmore's and Temple's are among them, but among the most prominent is that of the future Bishop Beadon of Bath and Wells. A spacious lawn leads out from the long range to the gatehouse on the road; its pebble paths still describe the triangular "ironing box" mentioned in *Lorna Doone*, and the letters P.B. are still picked out among the stones of the path near the gate.

The school had a stormy history from about 1840 to the 1870's, but in 1875 Augustus Lawrence Francis became headmaster and so remained for over forty years. His was a notable reign, for no event more so than for the move to the new buildings of 1880-2. Their style is Gothic, the main gateway is of some dignity, the architect was Hayward of Exeter. Now came the time for the alteration and conversion into dwelling-houses of the old range. Working from the east end, it had contained the Upper and Lower School divided by balustraded screen and gallery, a Hall, and the headmaster's house; the ushers had lived in a wing at the back. Now the long range was given floors and staircases. But still one can see the old trussed roof; a little of the screen survives as an umbrella stand; some Jacobean panelling is in what was the headmaster's house; there is still the shallow-arched fireplace that warmed the Hall.

Soon after the original Blundell's came the building, in St. Peter Street, of Chilcott's Free School which was founded in 1611. It is charming, of stone, with mullioned windows to light its single schoolroom and a rounded doorway like those of Old Blundell's or of the Great House of St. George that lies opposite and is a gabled, more elaborate essay in the same style; a rainwater head gives evidence of its date with its record of 1614.

The Great House of St. George is Tiverton's only good domestic building from before the eighteenth century; the frequent fires have seen to it that nothing else of so early a period remains. That of 1731 may have consumed much early Georgian work. But up and down there are still some excellent houses built between 1700 and 1850, while its varied buildings make St. Peter Street an excellent thoroughfare. There were also, at various times, the widenings out and "improvements" so common in Georgian England. We shall see how in 1783 a sad casualty was caused in Fore Street; in 1794 a Paving and Improvement Act led, no doubt, to more unquestion, ably good results.

St. Peter Street has many Georgian houses of various dates, most of them late in the period, but in one case of outstanding distinction as a minor work of the more Baroque phase of about 1710. Its front is a mixture of brick and stone, and over the door are brackets that support a delightful curved and broken pediment.

The other important district for Tiverton houses is Fore Street and there, despite the plate-glazed ground floors of buildings that are now shops, there is much worth seeing; one should not, for example, miss the brickwork and Ionic pilasters of about 1735, above Achille Serre's and the Chain Library. One house is dated 1736, and down Phoenix Lane a splendid house, now down at heel, has more brickwork and pilasters of about the same time. These replacements after the 1731 fire were soon made and in charming early Georgian provincial taste.

But the best house in Fore Street is the one that now houses the brewery offices of Messrs. Starkey, Knight, and Ford. This, too, its façade towering high above the other houses of the street, cannot be many years later than 1731; its Corinthian pilasters and heavy key, blocks are indications of an early Georgian date. At one time it was the home of the famous Sir John Duntze whose death was in 1830 (39).

Here and there in Tiverton proper we find Regency houses, but the best domestic work of the first half of last century is in Westexe. A quarter grew up to house the workers attracted by Heathcoat's factory, and such streets as Church Street and St. Paul Street are good and dignified in a late version of the Georgian tradition. For their houses, uniform in a greyish-pink brick and built about the 1840's, have round-headed doorways and keyblocks all round them in the manner of work done a century earlier (41). Some of Tiverton's best modern housing is also on this side of the river, to the left as one comes in from Bickleigh on the Exeter road.

From this industrial district it is an easy transition to the architecture of commerce. One must first return to the area of Fore Street. The market buildings are of no great note, but with the Market Cross it was far otherwise. It once stood in Fore Street itself, with the "shambles" for meat and fish running on towards the Town Hall. An older cross was burnt in 1731. It was soon replaced, at the expense of a merchant named William Upcott, by a structure of real distinction that only lasted, to Tiverton's grievous aesthetic loss, till 1783. I do not know who was its designer, but he achieved a true masterpiece among such buildings. It had a domed top and its main structure was held up by an eight-sided Roman Doric loggia whose sides were half of them straight, the other four fancifully concave in the manner of Archer's work at Birmingham Cathedral or of his Hill House at Wrest. The main room itself was a more conventional octagon, but the old engraving amply shows what a delight we have lost (8).

Tiverton's other important commercial grouping has also for the most part disappeared. But the factory was in its time a noble work of industrial architecture. It was built, as I have shown, as part of the movement in East Devon to retain trade (diminished by the collapse of Dutch export markets in the French Revolution) by grouping work in large factories that were more efficient than the old system of domestic weaving. Originally it was planned for cotton, but it was soon on woollens to take the place of those that had gone to the Netherlands. A few years later it was producing Heathcoat's lace.

The original builders were a firm called Heathfield and Dennis.

The contract was placed before the actual outbreak of war, on September 30th, 1791, the mason being William Gream of Ottery. The woodwork was to be by Edward Boyce, a local carpenter, the slating by William Green, the glazing by Joseph Howe, and the leadwork by George Johns. The result, as old prints show, was a six-storeyed building of towering dignity, the curve of its walls and cornice as they led towards its projecting wing being an anticipation of the "movement" popular with industrial architects today. Of this early work the one survival is the pair of Regency lodges. The early Victorian Gothic school, of 1841–3 and by the local architect G. A. Boyce, is from Heathcoat's time. For this "advanced" employer had come to rescue economic Tiverton in 1816. In another ten years he erected a water-wheel that was one of England's largest, and which needed a steam engine to boost it in dry weather when the leats had a poor head of water (canal-borne coal had come to Tiverton since 1814). We have seen, too, how the establishment was no less remarkable for its labour conditions than as a technical pioneer. Gream's building lasted till it was burnt down in the 1930's. Its successor is a brick block of obviously modern design and appearance.

Chapter VIII

CULLOMPTON

ALONE of our smaller East Devon towns, Cullompton, like Exeter, has always been on a main line of transport. For it lies along the Bristol–Exeter road, the main line of the railway runs easily past it to carry the trains, at speed, on their smooth run down from Burlescombe Tunnel and the county boundary, to the junction point of Exeter. The noise of trains, not obtrusive, is none the less in Cullompton a constant refrain. They are there, as is the town, because of the nature of the ground. For here, in the wide valley of the Culm, low enough down for a fair head of water yet not too near Exeter for Cullompton to be suburban to the city, is the obvious, richly fertile site for a thriving centre of agriculture and commerce. The one thing that Cullompton has lacked is striking events and famous personalities in its history.

The actual story is one of monastic ownership, of the influence in the town of various families of the local gentry, of a career in the woollen trade marked by constant rivalry between the two similarly occupied towns of Cullompton and Tiverton.

The manor in Saxon times was a royal possession, the parish was of large extent, with several hamlets, and so, as at Tiverton, arranged on a "collegiate" pattern. But we have seen how after the Conquest these church lands were soon made over to the new Abbey of Battle; in time they went, along with the gift of the living, to Battle's daughter priory of St. Nicholas at Exeter. All through the Middle Ages St. Nicholas' kept this patronage; it would seem also that the connection could take on a more personal form, for in 1522 one William Cullompton, presumably of a family in the town, became St. Nicholas' last prior.

The manor, too, became the property of a religious house. It had passed from royal hands to a succession of lay landowners, and in the end to Amicia, the Countess of Devon, whose daughter was the better known Isabella de Fortibus, whose activities we have

45 Cullompton: The Tower

47 Cullompton: Lane Aisle

46 Ottery: Outer North Aisle

FAN VAULTING, 1520-30

already noticed. Amicia, in 1278, was foundress of the Cistercian Abbey of Buckland in West Devon, and Cullompton was among the landed possessions with which she endowed the monks. The manor remained in their hands till the Dissolution in 1539; four years earlier it had been valued as the richest item in all their estates. So for all the later Middle Ages the Cistercian Abbots were lords of the manor in Cullompton. Remote they might be in point of distance, but they were not unmindful of the town's welfare, and it is to their bounty that we owe the most distinctively pleasing of all modern Cullompton's features. For in 1356 the Abbot put in hand the making of the watercourse that runs in across the fields from springs in the hill massif between Cullompton and Tiverton. By this agency a runnel of clear water, like that which the Countess Isabella had given to Tiverton, but in this case more widely distributed about the town, came in to give the dwellers in Cullompton a ready supply. On a smaller scale the Cullompton watercourse recalls Drake's leat which ran in, when Drake had brought it to Plymouth from the moorlands once owned by the Abbots of Buckland, to give Plymouth its first good water supply. It is curious to find that Drake's Cistercian predecessors at Buckland had in their own time done this very same thing for their manorial town on the other side of Devon.

With the Dissolution of the monasteries the manorial history of Cullompton became less notable than the commercial position of the town. Cullompton was already known for the making of stockings, Lane had been famous as a wool and cloth merchant; the story becomes mainly that of an East Devon textile town, with no single event of major importance, but with constant, eventually unsuccessful rivalry with Tiverton. There was migration from Tiverton to Cullompton after the former town's great fire in 1612, but Cullompton, with its less satisfactory head of water power for tucking mills, was always the smaller town of the two. For a time, however, in the nineteenth century, its woollens lasted on after the Tiverton trade had died down and given way to Heathcoat's. The leading figure in a brief period of factory production was one William Upcott, and the peak of Cullompton's population was reached, with a little less than 4,000 people, at the census of 1841.

But it is time now to make a survey of Cullompton as it is (the present population being about 3,000), and to start with its great glory, St. Andrew's Church, the best in Devon that has never had any but a parochial status.

St. Andrew's has no traces of Norman, or indeed of early Gothic architecture; apart from a thirteenth-century coffin-lid it is all Perpendicular, a memorial to the growing days of Cullompton's trade in wool and cloth. Where it is remarkable among Devon Perpendicular churches is in its beauty and dignity, in its kinship to the Somerset churches of the Taunton region, and in its obvious, mainly successful emulation of St. Peter's, Tiverton. Its proportions, especially in its clerestoried nave and chancel, give it a lofty, East Anglian feeling, enhanced by the rows of angels, their wings outstretched as on such hammerbeam roofs as those of Wymondham or March, that project from the cornice and from the bases of the principal rafters.

The nave is probably the oldest part of the church. Its arcades, six arches in each (with the eastern pair wider than the others), run continuously to divide the central space both from the nave aisles and from the chapels off the chancel. It may be that the nave and its clerestory are of the middle decades of the fifteenth century. The north aisle, with its excellent windows (some transomed, some with their lights uninterrupted) seems to have been walled anew and extended outwards about 1500 when the north chapel got its heraldic screenwork and became the chantry of the Moores. The south aisle, as we shall see, was drastically altered when John Lane gave the church its most notable addition. As at Tiverton the nave pillars have capitals carved with a delicate beauty not always found in Perpendicular churches. Some have foliage, other the heads and bodies of men, of widows, of kings, and of ladies whose "Ugly Duchess" headgear proclaims a date not far from 1450.

East of the nave is the chancel; it is not remarkable, being structurally part of the main fabric and not divided off by a chancel arch. Its history has a comic touch, for in the 1840's it was pulled down and rebuilt by William Froude, an engineer who had worked under Brunel on the building of the Bristol and Exeter railway. Froude was so convinced, albeit church and railway are several hundred yards apart, that the trains' vibration would damage the church, that he took this extreme precaution and also wished to take down the clerestory of the nave, and with it one of England's masterpieces of mediaeval woodwork.

For above all the main body of Cullompton church is the timber roof, designed and erected on the "cradle" pattern that is akin to the waggon or barrel-vaulted roof (51). It is a work of far more than average magnificence, with no parallels in Devon and Cornwall and few outside those counties. For every space between the cross rafters and those that run east and west is boarded over, the panels being given extra timbers that run from corner to corner. Each timber in the whole roof is richly edged with ornament, and at every intersection is a foliate boss; a few of the cross timbers are more massive than the others, more richly decorated, too, with elaborate wooden pendents. The whole impression is of a richness that anti-cipates the plasterwork or panelling of the Renaissance. One is accustomed to such roofing, on a limited scale, over sanctuaries or rood-lofts; here one has the treatment over a church's entire nave and chancel.

The liturgical subdivision of Cullompton Church was on the usual pattern, a screen across the building to cut off the chancel and chapels from the nave, and "parclose" screens to divide the chapels from the chancel. The screens, though not the other liturgical fittings of the east end, are with us now. The screen (51) is of the fifteenth century, of the usual Devon type that goes right across the church in one sweep with its traceried bays and richly foliate cornice. The vaulting that supports the loft is decked out with delicate little bosses, the main one in each bay being different from its fellows. Such a screen, however, is not rare in Devon. What is here so unusual is the pair of survivals from the rood, with its flanking figures, that stood on the screen to rivet the devotion of those who looked east from the nave as they assisted at Mass. The rood itself was not a hanging one, but above its place there is still the cross beam (51), specially ornate and with a lace-like delicacy of detail on its lower side, that would have had chains or ropes hanging down to the heads of the crosses; it would so have formed both a support and an upper framing to the devotional group below. The other survival, I think unique in England, is the heavily sculptured base, its carving piled up in a natural grouping, that still has the mortice holes for the crosses themselves. We see the skull and bones of Golgotha and the growing plants of spiritual rebirth; the work is clearly late mediaeval, but whatever its period the wonder remains.

West of the nave is the most splendid, and in its date the most disputable, feature of Cullompton Church. The tower would appear to have been built, and with success, as a rival to that at Tiverton. It has been assumed that this tower was built as late as the period 1545–9. But apart from the unlikelihood of so superb an addition to the church at a time of such religious unrest, with the Prayer Book Rebellion touching Devon deeply in the summer of 1549, the style of the tower seems to me to suggest a fifteenth-century date for at least part of its structure.

Cullompton tower (45), with its kinship to some in West Somerset and with its grouping, within Devon, along with those of Tiverton and Broad Clyst,* is akin to work done late in the fifteenth century. The west doorway, the carved decoration and the window above it, the shields and quatrefoils in Ham Hill stone round the lower stages, the buttresses and their projecting grotesques, the upper windows with their fretted, golden, Ham Hill stone, all these seem to be of a date before 1500 and not of the middle years of the six-teenth century. Finally come the elaborately pierced battlements and above them the corona of eight complex pinnacles, a little coarse in detail but giving to the tower a great richness which is unusual in Devon but more common in Somerset.

But the embellishments, a set of sadly worn Beer stone plaques let into the red sandstone masonry, are unmistakably mid-Tudor with flanking balusters in the Renaissance taste. The most important, perhaps set up about 1545 when it would still have been politically safe, is that of the Crucifixion, now mutilated, that is high up on the west face of the tower. There are also squat little figures of a king (Henry VIII or Edward VI?) and St. George, the Annunciation and the Tree of Life, the Tudor Royal Arms, episcopal and local heraldry. The plaques are an interesting enrichment, but not an outstanding artistic success.

* See F. J. Allen, *The Great Church Towers of England*, 1932, pp. 79–81 and plate 7.

There may, of course, have been some more thoroughgoing re⁄
construction, particularly of the upper stages, at the same time;
unfortunately the carved inscription on the west face is too worn to
be an effective piece of evidence and Bishop Veysey's Arms are only
on one of the plaques. But in 1545 we hear of a legacy for the "new"
(*novo*) tower of Cullompton. Yet "new" may have meant "reno⁄
vated", for the use of language over such matters as mediaeval
building work was often somewhat loose.* What I personally feel,
and here I know that I feel inclined to differ from so great an
authority as Professor Pevsner,† is that some at least of the tower's
structure is of the fifteenth century, that some of the older details may
perhaps have been reused when there was a reconstruction, and that
only the Beer stone embellishments are without a doubt of the 1540's.
The last, rather fussy addition to the tower was when the clock was
given its Gothic canopy in the 1870's.

The most perfect thing about Cullompton Church is the outer
south aisle of five bays, and presumably by the designer who worked
for Lady Wiltshire at Ottery, that was added about the 1520's by
the clothier John Lane.

The donor, who died in 1529, was in his own time the chief man
in Cullompton; unlike Greenway at Tiverton he had no king's
daughter to overshadow him in the social scale. Like Greenway he
was a rich woolman and cloth merchant. As steward or bailiff,
collecting their rents and dues for the Abbot of Buckland and the
Prior of St. Nicholas', he was, effectively speaking, the man on the
spot whose presence must have meant more to the townsmen than
the distant Cistercian Abbot.‡ Lane's wife was called Thomasine;
the chapel put up to serve as their chantry is even finer, in its way,
than the aisle at Ottery which it so much resembles. Its splendid
fan vault(47) has sculptured pendents (with little angels who hold
the Symbols of the Passion, other holy devices, and emblems of the
wool and cloth trades) that make it more elaborate than Lady

* See, in this connection, L. F. Salzman, in his *Building in England, Down to 1540*,
1952. The renovations to this tower are near enough to his terminal date for the same
considerations to apply.

† In his *South Devon*, Penguin "Buildings of England" series, 1952, p. 96.

‡ But the bailiff after Lane was the brother of Abbot Toker, the last abbot of
Buckland.

Wiltshire's vault. But the windows of the two aisles are similar and in both cases like those of Greenway's south aisle at Tiverton. At Cullompton the inner side of the fan vault rests, not on pillars of the ordinary type, but on piers whose northern sides become internal buttresses, so built perhaps as to give an impression of greater strength. Their sides are cleverly adorned with shallow, canopied niches that hold saintly or prophetic figures with scrolls. On the southern wall are statue brackets, and they and the corbels of the vault are liberally decorated, not with the noble heraldry of a great lady like the Countess of Wiltshire, but with angels, the Five Wounds, the Symbols of the Passion, the merchant's mark and the fleeces that betoken Lane the trader in wool.

The outside sculpture (44) of the aisle is so close a copy of Greenway's at Tiverton that it needs little description. There are the little carvings of scripture scenes, many of their subjects being exactly as at Tiverton, the initials J.L. and the tools of the cloth trade, Symbols of the Passion, anchors, and the admirable ships like those at Tiverton or on the famous bench-end at Bishop's Lydeard. But the general effect, though an older north porch is unhappily dwarfed, is more successful than in Greenway's chantry. One cannot well doubt that the carvers of the two chapels were the same concern. A long inscription calls piously, and only some twenty years in time, for paternosters and aves for John and Thomasine Lane, their children, their friends—Cullompton had said farewell in a blaze of glory to the liturgical splendours of the pre-Reformation church.

But Cullompton Church does not lack furnishings to prove that the adornment of churches did not cease with the Reformation. The Jacobean Holy Table is in the Lane aisle, and the finest relic of the early seventeenth century is the great western gallery with its slightly bulging Ionic columns, its Apostles and other saintly figures along the front, its friezes above and below the panels, its dainty little lions' masks, its initials C.P. and its pair of wool shears to link it with local trade. There are incised gravestones, some of the late Middle Ages, others to clothiers and merchants of succeeding centuries; the Georgian murals are without distinction, but one is to a midshipman of fifteen who fell in action, on March 14th, 1795, when Hotham and Nelson were in action with a French squadron in the Gulf of Genoa. There are the colours of the militia raised locally in the Napoleonic wars, and as we turn to another subject we find that the benefaction board is a good one of 1660; another that records later charities is in the Adam taste. Outside, the best ornaments are leaden rainwater heads in the Baroque vein; one is of 1709 and others are later by fifteen years.

There were no religious houses in pre-Reformation Cullompton; the one important charity of the period was an almshouse founded by John Trott in his will of 1523. The building remains, a long stone range at the Taunton end of the town. A Perpendicular doorway with carving in its spandrels is the only thing to indicate the date. This almshouse is humble enough, nor is there much to see in the non-Anglican places of worship. The Methodists and Baptists have late Georgian chapels (the former dated 1806) in the plainest of style; a better building is the chapel of 1830-1, set back from the Tiverton road with churchwarden Gothic windows and excellent iron railings, that was once that of the Congregationalists. Then for a time it had a career as the "Assembly Rooms" (Victoria Hall from the year of the Diamond Jubilee), and now it gives Cullompton an element of industry by being a branch factory of Heathcoat's.

Otherwise the older domestic buildings of Cullompton are mostly those of a place that long prospered as a clothing town, with fewer fires than other towns described in this book till the severe one of 1839. A variety of families took the place of Buckland Abbey as lords of the manor, but the emphasis is rather with those who carried on the local cloth trade.

There are two individual Cullompton houses of real note; otherwise the virtue of the place lies rather in the general impression it gives, particularly in the broad expanse, with limes along its sides and some good Georgian houses behind them, of High Street at the northern end of the town. There is the amazing profusion of "irrigated" streets, for tiny runnels from the watercourse run charmingly down every court and alley, and not only in the principal roads; they form a complex grid and add vastly to the distinction of Cullompton among the towns of England. There are the road names still racy of local custom—Lower and Upper Bull

Ring, Cockpit Hill, Pound Square, the New Cut, the courts like Jarman's or Matthews'. Of public buildings there are few. The shambles that once contained both butchery and market house were once narrow wooden buildings; in 1811 a new market house replaced them, a quaint little dated building in churchwarden Gothic that still exists with a shoe shop below its interlacing windows.

Cullompton's two best houses are Walrond's and "The Manor"; they lie close to each other on the western side of Fore Street. Each has an attractive garden at the back, and the main line of the water-course comes into the town through the land of the former.

The "Manor" House (only known as such for a century, and long called "Sellicks" from William Sellocke, an earlier owner) is dominantly placed at the corner of the Tiverton road. Its front is mostly late Tudor or early Jacobean, but inside and at the back there was heavy remodelling about 1718.

The façade (48), mostly of timber and plaster and beneath four gables, is built between conspicuous end walls of stone like those of Elizabethan houses in Exeter or Plymouth. On them are plaques, one with initials that may be of Thomas Trock and his wife, the other dated 1603. The windows, with their wooden mullions and transom timbers, are supported on typical carved brackets, there are little Ionic pillarets, and a decorated cornice to part the first and second storeys. But the striking thing about the house is its main doorway. It must have been put in when many other changes were made about 1718, for it has a "shell" hood, and within that hood a striking double shell of naturalistic design. It is so much like one at Topsham of the same date that the two doors seem surely to be by the same hand, perhaps a Topsham plasterer who knew the sea-shore and took his designs from what he picked up. But the hood must have proved too heavy, for later in the century the doorway was given supporting pillars and a fanlight that makes it an intriguingly composite achievement. Within, the Manor House has no Tudor features, but an early Georgian staircase, and in one of the rooms the panelling and bolection mouldings of the same period. At the back, the outside of the stairway projection has the same blue and red brickwork that we have seen already at Tiverton Castle; here, too,

48   Cullompton: "Manor House", *c.* 1603

49   Tiverton: Old Blundell's, 1604

50 Tiverton:
The Nave

51 Cullompton: The
Nave and Chancel

is the rainwater head of 1718 that dates the remodelling of the house.

Walrond's is wholly different, in its plan and style more like a country manor than a town house. Here, too, the name is not original, for a Walrond was not the owner till about 1790. The actual builders, about 1603–5, were the Petres. The house is of stone, with two projecting wings to flank a central doorway, a wealth of mullioned windows, and pinnacles, of a pyramid type, to crown its gables. Inside, the hall has an elaborate chimney-piece with the date 1605 and an achievement of the Petre arms; better still is another heraldic overmantel upstairs, and in the same room is the best of the house's pleasant group of ribbed and foliate plaster ceilings. In one of the wings a parlour has inlay to embellish its panelling, and among the attics of the other wing a room is said to have been the Mass Room, in penal times, of the house's Catholic occupants.

One cannot claim outstanding merit for the rest of Cullompton's houses, though the churchyard has on one side a long row, one of its houses thatched, that may go back as far as the Tudors. Along the line of Fore Street and then High Street is a variety of eighteenth-century fronts, in the Half Moon and White Hart Inns, for example, and the delightful house, of about 1780, with its double-bowed front and mellow red brick, that now houses the electricity offices. The courts and alleys have a "quaintness" and charm of their own, and New Street, rebuilt after the fire of 1839, runs straight from the main road and comes as an excellent, simply-designed example of a small-town street that even at so late a date continued to embody the Georgian tradition. It leads towards the district of Shortlands, and there, used now for other purposes than cloth, the mill building that was run by William Upcott is a simple, unpretending piece of industrial architecture.

Chapter IX

TOPSHAM AND EXMOUTH

THE seaward end of the Exe valley has as its two chief towns a pair of sharply contrasted communities, one with a long history as a port, the other mainly concerned with the business of recreation. For Topsham, though now a yachting rather than a commercial haven, and increasingly a place of residence and retirement, has an aspect and an architecture essentially those of an old maritime town. Exmouth, with the history of a fishing village and with a dock that plies more trade than Topsham quay, has overwhelmingly the appearance of a Regency, and then Victorian seaside resort.

Topsham is well up the estuary, with its waterfront overlooking a narrow channel rather than lying upon a sweeping tidal expanse (55), and owing its beauty in large measure to its distant prospects and to its almost East Anglian blend of old buildings and picturesque aquatic activity. It is, moreover, a peninsular town with another river at its back. For although it has always been more aware of the Exe than of the Clyst, it is placed only a little above the point where the latter river, after a course beset with meanderings, and liable for that reason to turgid floods, runs down to the larger estuary. The bridge of Topsham, of five arches and probably in its present form a Georgian work, and the rambling, externally Georgian but by origin much older Bridge Inn, are both at the spot where the Clyst is crossed by the road from Exeter via Topsham that continues to Exmouth.

As the Romans realised, Topsham was made by Nature as the obvious port for Exeter. For there by the quay the deep-water channel of the Exe made the last embarking point that could, without intense and perhaps disproportionate human endeavour, be made available to seagoing craft. I do not know what the Romans called the port of *Isca Dumnoniorum*, and the name of Topsham itself seems to refer to the "ham" of some Saxon whose name included the syllable "top". But the town's history has always been nautical, firstly a long period, with the port not at first made obsolete by the cutting of Exeter's boat canal, as the effective harbour of Exeter, then a career as a coasting port which was also a considerable builder of wooden sailing ships. The first period also saw some manufacturing activity, in addition to the town's great trade with the Netherlands, for a glasshouse of the type common in Bristol was at work near Topsham about 1700* (see page 162). The second phase was more important in the Napoleonic Wars (with a 22-gun man-o'-war built at Topsham in 1806) and continued more than half-way through the nineteenth century; it included repairs and drydocking as well as shipbuilding and the use of the quay.

It is therefore no surprise that Topsham's best aspect is in its buildings of a domestic or nautical character. Those buildings are mainly found in Fore Street, which is the continuation of the way in from Exeter; they are also lower down in Ferry Road (originally, and more graphically, known as "Underway"), in the quay, the Strand, and in side streets running inland in the southern part of the town. The church is well placed on its eminence, its graveyard overlooking the river and bounded by a lofty wall (rebuilt in 1805) that falls sheer to a section of "Underway". But the building itself, as we shall see, is no longer of major note, though among its monuments it contains the best artefact in Topsham.

The nautical flavour of Topsham is best expressed, as one would expect, by the long riverside road that runs north and south along the low ground by the Exe; it starts at the top of Ferry Road, continues past the quay, and ends past the Dutch-style house fronts that are the distinctive feature of the Strand; at one time the whole of the Strand was closer than now to the water's edge. The quay, with little use made of it, but a delightfully placed, breezy expanse, gives the best of Topsham's views on to the river and an easy prospect over the yachts, sailing dinghies, and other pleasure craft that now frequent the tidal stream; over the river a narrow expanse of meadow parts the Exe from the lowermost reach of the Exeter Canal.

So far as buildings go, the main relics of Topsham's nautical

* See W. A. Thorpe, *History of English and Irish Glass*, vol. I, p. 143.

history are the warehouses and building sheds. For in the lower section of Ferry Road there are warehouses, probably some two centuries old, and houses whose ground floors are storing places for merchandise or sails. The relics of Topsham's shipbuilding are more widely spread. At the extreme north of Ferry Road one still sees a capacious wet dock, and near it a long building shed that is now a house with windows in mediaeval style. Another shed of similar type is in the Strand and opposite the "Dutch" houses. A dry dock, too, was also here; the yard was one of those in use by Holman's, the Topsham firm that carried on the industry and built sailing ships in Victorian days.

Topsham's best old houses are of the seventeenth and eighteenth centuries, with some whose date-range takes us down to the 1840's. The best way to study them is to work southwards from the Exeter side of the town, thus finishing at the lower end of the Strand where the prospect of the wider estuary looks seaward in the direction of Exmouth.

The dominant buildings in High Street and Fore Street are houses, shops, and inns.

The best of Topsham's Georgian, a stately house that dates early in the period, perhaps from about 1740, is the one called Broadway House, its solid front in mellow red brick having a pedimented door with fluted Ionic pilasters, all behind excellent wrought-iron gates; it must always have belonged to some leading man in Topsham and now houses a doctor. Lower down, in Fore Street, are some late eighteenth-century houses in red brick "Exeter Georgian", a Regency shop front with pilasters and Ionic pillars, and nearer to the church a good piece of very late eighteenth-century brickwork in Cromer House. A turn off Fore Street takes us into Follett Street, and there we have Clara Place, a delightful little three-sided court of nine "Regency" houses whose date is actually 1841.

Back in Fore Street the Globe Inn, too, is Georgian, but Fore Street's most notable adornment is the projecting porch of the "Salutation". Of the 1720's, and thrusting out into the highway, it is curious for the unorthodoxy, a blend of Venetian window and interrupted pediment, of its window design, a dash of vernacular Palladian in a provincial seaport town. Down by the water the

52 Exmouth: The
Temple, 1824

53 Topsham: Duckworth
Monuments, by Chantrey

54   The Passage Inn

55   From across the Exe

TOPSHAM

Passage Inn is another old house of vernacular character, its front slate-hung, its doorway pedimented, and on the building a plaque with the name of T. N. Parker and a date (later than the inn itself) of July 12th, 1788 (54).

The central section of the Topsham waterfront is largely made up of the quay and there, set back from the facing wall, is a building that combines an old Custom House and the Lighter Inn, its name an echo of transhipments from Exeter along the canal. The building has gables of the seventeenth century, and set in the chimney-stacks, as in other Topsham stacks, are some of the thin little Dutch bricks that came as ballast in ships from the Netherlands.

One comes from the quay to the streets of houses—Higher and Lower Shapter Street, Monmouth Street, and Monmouth Hill, that lead away from the line of the Strand or run parallel to its course. Conway House in Lower Shapter Street is of the middle years of the eighteenth century and has fine tiled fireplaces, while Monmouth Hill has single-storey houses that remind me of equivalents in Ireland. But Monmouth Street, with its little pillared porches and generally Georgian effect, is the best of the group.

The Strand starts well with a house whose rainwater head is dated 1718, and whose door has a hood and a double shell, exactly imitated from Nature, whose artistic blood-brother we have seen at Cullompton. Then, as one goes southwards, comes the "picturesque" and therefore residential sector of the Strand, the area of the five Dutch gables.

The houses themselves are of mainly eighteenth-century date, and a pair without Dutch character, named Estuary Villas, are pleasing "Regency". But here, as nowhere else in the lower Exe valley, is visual proof of the Dutch connection in the peak period of the cloth trade when the Hollanders bought East Devon serges for their own wear and to forward up the Rhine to the eager markets of central Europe. Whether they were occupied by English traders under Dutch influence, or by Dutch agents and factors living temporarily in Devon (there were others, Katencamps for instance, and Steen-wycks, who stayed and founded a Devon colony of Anglo-Dutch), the reason for those stepped and curving gable-ends is unmistakable. What we have here to do, bearing in mind that Rotterdam rather than Amsterdam was the chief Dutch reception port, is to assess their merit. Viewed as Dutch architecture they are minor works, for all their beauty of outline. In Devon they are charming exotics, in East Anglia they would be less surprising, but they cannot be classed as outstanding specimens by those who know Delft or Leiden, or have browsed among the tree-lined, architecturally amazing *grachten* of Amsterdam.

The church at Topsham still has, on its south side, a simple Perpendicular tower with a panelled arch. Otherwise it is all in the Gothic of the 1870's, the architect for this complete rebuilding being Ashworth of Exeter. But the bowl-shaped font is Norman, with decoration in an incised pattern and a pleasant little lion carved on its eastern side. There are the Royal Arms of Charles II and a collection of late Georgian mural monuments, of flags, and of hatchments, that must have made of the older church a picturesque sight till Ashworth got to work on it. Then in the south transept a group of memorials to the Duckworths combine artistic merit and historic interest.

The family of Admiral Sir John Duckworth was settled at Topsham by the years of the Regency, and though Sir John died as Commander in Chief, Plymouth, in 1817, he is commemorated here in Topsham. His *stele* is by Chantrey, and upon it the bust of the Admiral has Grecian drapery, but upon the folds is pinned the star of the G.C.B.! The sides have wreathed tridents, a flag bears the list of the Admiral's chief actions, and in front is a graphic relief, surely to be classed among the better scenes of naval warfare so immortalised, of Duckworth's principal victory, the action off San Domingo in 1806. By the side of this monument another by Chantrey is to the Admiral's son, Lieutenant-Colonel George Henry Duckworth, who fell at Albuera in 1811. The officer is shown in uniform, and an angel with a trumpet crowns him with a wreath (53). His sister too is remembered by a simpler and unsigned tablet. She married into the navy, her husband being Rear-Admiral Sir Richard King, who was peacetime Commander-in-Chief on the East Indies Station. Lady King, née Sarah Anne Duckworth, took passage to join him in the *Minden*, 74, but on March 20th, 1819, she died at sea and was buried when the warship made port at

Bombay. It is a wistful picture, the reverse of the numerous sea passages harmlessly enjoyed by so hardened a naval wife as Jane Austen's Lady Croft.

A few modern buildings can end our perambulation of Topsham. The Roman Catholic church, not far from the station, was started in 1936. It is a pleasant little building, in simple brickwork of a restrained colour, with a campanile at one corner and a generally Romanesque idiom. To revert at the last to the Dutch connection, one notices, on some of the modern council houses, that there are twentieth-century versions of the Dutch gables which have given Topsham a place of distinctive renown among the towns of the West.

One enters Exmouth from the north, and through parts of the town that once belonged to the parish of Withycombe Raleigh. One sees at a glance that Exmouth is a considerable place; with a population over 17,000 it is indeed by far the largest of the seaside places between Weymouth and Torquay. A great part of it, including the area to the north of the station, is on land reclaimed from the salt marshes of the estuary.

The southern, or seaward end of Exmouth is what must chiefly concern us, and there the natural outline still betokens the time when what is now in the main a seaside resort was, to quote Leland, "a fisschar tounlet, a little within the havyn mouthe". The estuary comes down from Topsham in a broad, unspoilt expanse, but it does not reach the English Channel direct. For the projecting sandbars, Dawlish Warren on the western side, on the other the low-lying part of Exmouth itself, thrust out from their respective banks, outflank each other, and so divert the last stretch of the Exe that this river, having run north and south for over thirty miles, now flows west to east as it finally embraces the sea. So Exmouth's beach is unusual in that the swift current of a river flows lengthways past its sands. Above the beach, a low cliff rises to the green expanse and Georgian terrace of the Beacon; the height above the sea is modest, yet enough to ensure that an artist like Danby would have been captured by the beauty of the landscape—the last reach of the Exe, beyond the river the Haldon Hills, and then Dawlish with its familiar red cliffs to lead the eye along to the broken skyline which is the northern arm of Torbay.

I have said that what is now the seaside area was once a hamlet or chapelry in Littleham parish; the manor itself was the property in the Middle Ages of the Benedictines of Sherborne Abbey. The chapel was dedicated to the Holy Trinity; nothing of it remains, nor yet of its successor that was built in 1779 and "redecorated" in 1810. A larger rebuilding was in the 1820's, with the new chapel consecrated in 1824. It seems that some pillars from that rebuilding may be in the present Holy Trinity, a large, far seen, dignified church, Edwardian Perpendicular with a lofty pinnacled tower; its designer was George Fellowes Prynne. But the best of Exmouth's church architecture is still at Littleham, two miles east of the larger place.

The chancel has thirteenthcentury traces, and its chapel has two low arches, without capitals, of the century that followed. The remainder fits the usual Devon pattern of Perpendicular rebuilding. The simple west tower seems likely to be of the fifteenth century, but the excellent north arcade, with its four arches, was started as late as Henry VIII's reign and is a contemporary of the more elaborate aisles at Ottery and Cullompton. The best of the church's old furnishings for worship are the late mediaeval screen, the altar rails of the early eighteenth century, and the really admirable early Tudor glass; the comparatively rare St. Roche is there along with St. Michael and Christ showing the Five Wounds.

The monuments remind us that Littleham was still the church for Exmouth in the early days of the resort, for several are to invalids who died at Exmouth between 1790 and about 1840; a parishioner commemorated is a mariner named Henry Stafford (d. 1746), whose memorial has a relief of a fullrigged ship. But the best known, an accompaniment to her grave in the churchyard, is Turnerelli's to Lady Nelson. A Grecian woman mourns over a double tomb, for the memorial also commemorates Lady Nelson's son by her first husband, the undistinguished Captain Josiah Nisbet, who died a year before his mother, in 1830. The sculptured tomb bears the Arms of Nisbet and a lozenge with a coronet over N for Nelson. The tablet was put up by Nisbet's widow, "in grateful remembrance of those virtues which adorned a kind mother-in-law and a good husband".

Exmouth's port area is at the western end of the town; one has to go there for the ferry that plies across the estuary roadstead to Starcross. The area has not much to show, and the cargo basin is unimpressive. The main thing is that it exists and that here, in addition to Exmouth's more modern activity as Exeter's specially popular bathing place, and as a resort of national popularity, one has continuity with the town's longer past as a haven.

The return towards Exmouth's Regency area is by way of the sea wall, a fine piece of sloping stonework that was started in 1841 with John Smeaton as its engineer. The Clock Tower, useful as such erections are apt to be, and, artistic merits apart, a popular object as clock towers often become (witness Plymouth and Leicester), was put up in 1897. Behind it are the gardens of the Imperial Hotel, above it the slopes and terraces of the Beacon; with them we are in the part of Exmouth most worth seeing by the lover of good building.

The lower, more sheltered part of the town has late Georgian houses in the Parade (started about 1790) and in the triangle known as the Strand. But both have lost much of their earlier character by rebuilding or by the coming of plate-glass shop fronts. They have also lost many buildings, the Globe Inn for instance and Exmouth's first theatre, that were important when the town first became much visited as a resort. The same is true of the area closer to the Beacon, for the original Assembly Rooms no longer perform their first function, and one of Exmouth's two pseudo-Athenian buildings has also gone. This was a supposed replica, in the Manor gardens, of the Tower of the Winds. But there is still the curious little lodge built in 1824 as a pretended reproduction in miniature of the Theseum. Its porch and "transepts" are, of course, Victorian additions, and as the space between the two central columns of its portico is more than those between the others, it is not exactly the pure Doric of the fifth century B.C. (52), yet it contrives to be not least among the architectural attractions of Exmouth. Moreover, enough remains, in addition to the "Temple", to give a good impression of Exmouth, the first in date of East Devon's seaside towns; it is worth remembering that its growth was earlier than that of Sidmouth.

For the least altered part of Exmouth one needs to climb to the Beacon, and then behind it and Holy Trinity to drop back by way of such simple, seemly, brick-built streets as Bicton Place with its neat little Georgian cottages. At the foot of our ascent, on a rounded corner at the foot of Beacon Hill, a house that is now a pharmacy has a porch, a bow window, and corner windows curved to correspond to the house's shape, the windows being divided up by the slenderest of columns, the whole a delightful essay in "Regency" taste.

The houses on the Beacon were started, the lowest first, in 1792; the row continues till the later "Regency" group, with shutters thrown back from the windows against the creamy background of the stucco, of Louisa Terrace whose eastward ending is an admirable separate villa. The oldest houses have pedimented doorways of a character that is clearly "builder's Georgian". They and some others are in mellow red brick, other have stucco fronts, and there are Ionic doorways and porches (57). A stretch of mown grass extends along the whole of the Beacon like a ribbon of green; from their upper windows the houses have the view that an early guide-book to British watering places* noted as being "by many persons deemed the finest in England". It was here on the Beacon that Lady Nelson and the second Lady Byron had their lodgings; by way of contrast Mary Anne Clarke had dwelt only a short distance away. The houses are still named Nelson House and Byron Court.

We must say farewell to Exmouth by the way of our approach, for near the road, on northern slopes that look over the town and across the estuary, is a group of buildings of national significance among out architecture of the odd and eccentric.

They are the polygonal house known as "A La Ronde", the Point in View Chapel, which combines in one block four alms-houses and a tiny Nonconformist chapel, and the Manse. They were built to a plan, and in pursuit of a "point in view", that make them the most unusual buildings which Exmouth, or indeed the whole district, can show.

* A Guide to all the Watering and Sea-Bathing Places, etc. London, 1810.

The ladies who built the house, whom one cannot but compare in their more bourgeois way to those of Llangollen, were of Devon middle-class stock, the Misses Jane and Mary Parminter, whose period of main activity was between 1795 and about 1805. They were well-to-do, they had travelled in Mediterranean countries, they had formed unusual religious and benevolent ideas. Their first step, the model in mind being the Ravenna church of San Vitale, was to build themselves a sixteen-sided house, mainly of stone, but with brick chimneys and a thatched, conical roof. This, with its lofty hall running up to a gallery, and with decorations to say the least of it unusual in a permanent residence, was to be their home. Higher up, and after the house had been finished, they founded an almshouse whose conditions of entry enshrined views they had formed on the crying need for the conversion of the Jews. For among the four poor spinster women who were to be its inmates one was to act as mistress for six girls attending a school incorporated in the building; she was to be chosen, for preference, from Jews who had embraced Christianity. The same basis of selection was to apply to the parents of the children themselves. Moreover, some oaks on the estate were not, so runs the story, to be felled till the Jews were due to return to Palestine; it has been said that their timber was to be used to help build the ships required for a mass immigration. The almshouse and its chapel continue their functions, but one hears less now, for practical reasons, of the Parminter ladies' conditions. Where A La Ronde and Point in View are perennially remarkable is as architectural and decorative oddities.

The house was built in 1795-8 and is not, as I found when at Ravenna, much like San Vitale; it lacks, for instance, all traces of internal arcading and the exterior likeness, too, is somewhat far-fetched. It has also been much altered, for the tiled roof and dormer windows are modern (56). The fenestration of this most extraordinary of *Cottages ornées* is its most novel outside feature. For the windows of the ground-floor storey (the lowest of all were made to light the basement) are rectangular with shutters and of a diamond shape, and they occur not in the flat spaces but on the actual corners of the sixteen-sided polygon.

Within, the scene is more curious and more bizarre. The central hall rises some forty feet to its gallery and upper lantern; off it lead the living-rooms, some of them constrained by the angles and plan of the building to be of curious shapes, awkward to carpet, clean, and furnish. There are many curios, in particular of shellwork that was some of it made with shells gathered by the Misses Parminter on the local beaches, and much of the furniture, among it a table dated 1802, has always been in the house. Some rooms have painted valances over their windows, an intricately worked drawing-room cornice of feather work has kept its brilliant colours, while decora-tion in feathers is also round a drawing-room door.

The upper gallery and its approaching staircase are the strangest curios in this truly original house; here, perhaps, in their intricately designed and coloured decoration of shells and feathers, we may trace the Byzantine influence of San Vitale's mosaics. For between the uppermost gallery windows with their lattice panes are geometrical designs in shellwork with a cornice above. More conspicuous are the panels of featherwork depicting a series of sadly decayed birds. A parrot is the best preserved; the bright green of his plumage sug-gests that his own species contributed or that there were heavy casualties among the Exmouth woodpeckers. This upper embellish-ment must have taken the ladies some years to achieve, for a large royal crown has with it the date of 1809.

The chapel was finished in 1811, the year of Jane's death; it was licensed for services the next year. Mary Parminter lived till 1849, and both ladies are buried there. The tiny chapel, with its organ and reading-desk compactly combined as one piece of furniture, was once confined to the space below its little spire. But now it includes the area of the minister's first lodging, and its vestry was the school-room for the six little girls. The four almshouse cottages are cast round the central spirelet and so complete the block; their windows have the same criss-cross pattern of glazing that one finds in the main house. Behind the chapel is the Manse of 1829. Its plan is that of a compact, neat little Regency villa. But here, too, the windows have the diamond pattern made by their glazing bars, and one has a diamond shape like the smaller windows in A La Ronde. These Parminter ladies pursued their architectural oddities, like their philo-Jewish "point in view", with considerable persistence.

56   A La Ronde, 1795-8

57   The Beacon, 1792 and later

GEORGIAN EXMOUTH

58   In High Street

59   In Weir Barton Road

Exeter: Post-war

Chapter X

CRESCENT PHOENIX

ONE cannot claim outstanding distinction for architecture in Exeter between the wars. The two main stations each saw considerable changes, for Central was rebuilt by the Southern Railway in the early 1930's, being given a smart, well-shaped street building that was a respectable essay in brick and stone "Queen Anne". At St. David's the Great Western were less sweeping, but gave the station a plain propylaeum to mask part of Brunel's long Italianate façade. The University College, its earliest separate building in Gandy Street an essay in the "Wren" taste, increased its buildings, already swollen by the taking over of some Georgian houses amid Exeter's hilly northern outskirts. The main element in the additions was Reed Hall, its situation magnificently commanding, its idiom that of the neo-Renaissance so dear in those years to those who sought an alternative to Gothic. There were churches, too, in various parts of the suburbs; of these the most exciting to my mind is the Roman Catholic one of the Blessed Sacrament at Heavitree, with its Corinthian portico at one side and a basilican classic interior in varied marble. There were houses, too, in great numbers, none better than some along and just off the Topsham road. They have about them a flavour of Welwyn Garden City, which is no surprise when one knows that the architect for both places was the same.

Then in early May 1942 the Exeter raids were part of the "Baedeker" series loosed on some of our historic cities. They were moderate compared with the weight of attack on such industrial or seaport centres as Coventry or Liverpool. But for a city of Exeter's size they were a severe blow; the damage was less dramatic than in Plymouth, but it was more spectacular, if only because much of the shopping centre was affected, than at Bath. But now there are parts of the city whose restoration has gone far enough for the centre of Exeter to show a collection of buildings that is largely new. There are also districts where architecture has arisen on previously empty ground.

The most evident devastation was mostly along the line of Exeter's main thoroughfare from Sidwell Street to Fore Street, with more damage on the southern and eastern than on the western and northern sides of the road. There was also severe injury to Georgian terraces in and near Southernhay, the saddest casualty being most of Dix's Field. By the river, and in the railway and industrial districts, the damage was comparatively slight. But up in the old city there were three patches of what one may call "area devastation". They were in the direction of Sidwell Street, a sector in and off High Street that included, most tragic of all, the whole of Bedford Circus, and a space where South Street comes up to the crossroads with Fore Street and High Street and where the steady descent to the river begins. The second of these is the one where most has been done to fill in the open space with buildings of our own century.

The method has been for the city to obtain the bombed sites by compulsory acquisition, and then for plots to be leased to those wishing to build anew; many previous occupiers, banks for instance, and insurance companies, have taken leases so as to ensure their return to this most central and convenient part of Exeter. But it has not followed that new work has kept, or will keep, to the old alignment of streets and roads. Exeter, rebuilding now with considerable speed and an important example of a bombed English city in course of rebirth, has a more recognisable centre than the new Plymouth, but none the less the changes in plan are very considerable.

The entrance from Taunton or London is hardly started, but it will have a large, somewhat curiously aligned open space to be known as Eastgate Square; among its facilities it will include some subways for pedestrians and perhaps a large sunk garden. Then comes the new High Street, already in large measure complete, and without doubt in its basic plan an improvement on the congested roadway that was there before. There is, however, an unbombed sector that follows where Exeter's long famous traffic congestion continues to exist. But High Street in its new spaciousness reminds me of the Georgian Tything at Worcester where relative ease and space succeed the awkward narrowness of Foregate Street. Of the buildings, as of others newly erected in central Exeter, I shall speak later.

A far greater change has come over the area once pleasantly filled, and in a well-planned manner, by Bedford Circus. Complete as was the destruction of Bedford Chapel and all the houses, I cannot help being sorry that the planners of the new Exeter did not perpetu-ate the shape of this, the city's most attractive Georgian feature. But what they have laid out on its site and just to the north is the most novel item so far started as part of the rebuilding.

Some temporary shops in Eastgate, run up to meet some of Exeter's urgent shopping needs, and leading off High Street so as to face a section of the city walls that the bombing had exposed, had proved how pleasant, in the manner of the Calverstraat at Amster-dam, is the "non vehicular" shopping street. So Mr. Rowe, the city architect, has planned to give Exeter a more permanent version of the idea in Princesshay that is to run diagonally across the central area of war destruction. It is to be so aligned as to give a vista exactly to the north tower of the Cathedral; at its southern end is Bedford Street which continues now in an unbroken line past the site of Deller's and over that of Bedford Circus to the upper end of Southernhay. But hardly any buildings in Princesshay had been started by the late days of September 1952, only at its upper end a few shops existed at the back of a larger, V-shaped block whose more important frontage is on to High Street.

The bombed tract of ground near Sidwell Street is to have shops and light industry, and shops are to be in that near South Street which now includes the ruins of the Lower Market. But here as yet there is little new to see; the achievements to date are in the central area of devastation.

By the end of September 1952, the future aspect of at least a part of this redeveloped area was finally, and not in all ways happily, clear. The buildings finished were nearly all along the main street; in Bedford Street much had been done on two banks, but nothing was visible of Exeter's future G.P.O. The idea underlying the view of the Cathedral to be enjoyed by the sauntering shoppers of Princesshay can best be appreciated by sitting in the little enclosure marked by the plaque unveiled on October 21st, 1949, by our present Queen (hence Princesshay). But the main interest in what has been done lies in the elevations and styles of the buildings wholly or nearly complete.

The lessees of the various plots have all been free to choose their own designs and to dictate their style. Their liberty of choice might in certain circumstances have produced interesting and, indeed, excellent results; there is no need in street architecture for the invariable application of the methods of exterior control that gave us the stylistic uniformity of Wood the Younger's Royal Crescent at Bath; Ludlow and Lewes, for instance, are sermons to the contrary. But the new Exeter at present seems likely to be a durable monument to the stylistic chaos and indeterminism of mid twentiethcentury England, and to the all too frequent unreadiness of architects and clients to build boldly in such twentiethcentury style as we have evolved. It so far seems that we are not in Exeter to have that tonic breath of the contemporary which the Dolcis Shoe Company have given to otherwise uninspired new streets in Plymouth and Bristol. It appears, from what has now been completed, that the creators of the new Exeter are somewhat too heavily in debt to the admittedly good Georgian architecture already in the city; there is a Georgian flavour of well entrenched brickcumfreestone even in the more contemporary of the new façades.

If one starts from Sidwell Street, the first new building, that of Marks and Spencer's, is perhaps the best, and certainly the most positive in its style, of those by now in use (58). It is also an admirably conceived building in which to shop. Its main defect seems to me to be its somewhat illbalanced street front. Nearly opposite is the tame, though reasonably contemporary block, with offices and small shops in the same building and its back elevation a part of Princesshay, put up for Ravenseft Properties; the entrance to mediaeval Exeter's underground water conduits is just behind. But farther down the main street, on the same side as Marks and Spencer's, covering the site of St. Lawrence's Church and preserving in its hall the statue of Elizabeth I that once stood on the conduit head and then on the church porch, is a sequence of buildings that will no doubt be convenient and useful but which well epitomise the aesthetic tragedy of our times.

The range starts with the offices of one insurance company, con﹍ tinues with those of another insurance company, and then with Lloyd's Bank in a raised central block. It ends, at a lower elevation, with more shops that run almost to the beginning of the mock﹍ Tudor territory in the middle sector of High Street. The upper part of the range, including the central portion with a lofty entrance arch, is "Wrenaissance" that might perhaps have seemed a little daring in the days of Martin Shaw. Then this row of buildings that might have been a uniform, if outmoded, unity takes a stylistic jump of about forty years and becomes "modern" in the shops that include the premises of Messrs. Montague Burton. The result is not one of which a town of Exeter's quality, least of all a town that once possessed Bedford Circus, has any reason to be proud; it is as if the mauling of Carlton House Terrace or Berkeley Square (London not Bristol) had been done by original Georgian and not by modern designers.

It remains to note that St. Mary Arches has been sensitively and tastefully restored, that the structural renovation of the Cathedral is nearly complete, and that the choir now has a new pulpit given by the Free Churches of Exeter. One appreciates their idea, but it seems a pity, when one remembers the capacities of some modern artists, that it had to be similar in design and detail to the pulpits adorned by the eloquence of fifteenth﹍century parish priests in some neighbouring Devon villages.

The architecture of mid twentieth﹍century Exeter is unquestion﹍ ably happier where it has been allowed to rise on virgin soil. Well over two thousand houses, most of them of "traditional" materials, but not all in long established styles, have been built since 1945. There are some of the usual or expected accompaniments—schools, shops, a block of old people's homes at Stoke Hill, in an older part of the city an excellent modern factory at Marsh Barton. Light in﹍ dustry and the expansion of University College are both provided for, but it does not seem that the city will go much more than ten thousand beyond its 1951 population, according to the preliminary census return, of 75,479.

One may take as examples the buildings by now planned or started, or in some cases finished, between the Topsham road and the low ground by the river. Not far south of the Barracks, and close to the excellent houses of the late 1930's, a secondary modern girls' school has been designed and finished in a manner not uncommon with similar buildings whose construction is along "traditional" and not "aluminium prefabricated" lines; it stands at the bottom of Earl Richard's Road, the name commemorating the Richard de Redvers who confirmed the foundation of the nearby priory of St. James. Farther on, past the turning to Countess Weir bridge, and so below Countess Weir itself and about half-way from the city to Topsham, is the Countess Weir estate. One reaches the heart of it by turning down Glasshouse Lane, at the bottom are a farm, some old thatched cottages, a larger house, and the remains of the furnaces that ventured on the glass trade in the early years of the eighteenth century (see page 143). The estate had one school finished and one just started in the early autumn of 1952, an excellent block of small shops was completing and many of the roads of houses had all their inhabitants. The houses are a mixture; some are prefabricated in the Swedish manner, others are "Cornish Unit", others, and in appearance the best, are "traditional" in their construction, but are not too much committed to neo-Georgian design or details (59). One sees them well in such a section of the estate as Weir Barton Road; many have charming porches in light woodwork, and their brick is of a pleasing hue. The view is excellent across fields to the hills of Haldon. Behind the houses are tall trees, for the scene is well diversified, both amid the houses and in the balks which separate the carriageways from the main highway of the road to Topsham and Exmouth, by great elms allowed to stand as ornaments of the housing area. Some of them rest on foundations which are the small surviving fragments of typical Devon hedges.

INDEX

The numerals in heavy type denote figure numbers of illustrations

51